SO-BNE-875

# WHAT TO
# EXPECT
## WHEN **ADOPTING**
# D🐾G

WITHDRAWN

GUIDE TO **SUCCESSFUL DOG ADOPTION**
FOR EVERY FAMILY

# DIANE ROSE-SOLOMON

SOP3 Publishing
1507 7th Street #420
Santa Monica, CA 90401

For information about special discounts for bulk purchases, please contact info@SOP3.com

Book design by Nate Myers, wilhelmdesignco.com
Editing by Misty Cook, logophileediting.com
Chapter illustrations by Lisette Rotman, lisetteart.com
Front and back cover photos courtesy:
Shelter Me Photography www.facebook.com/ShelterMePhoto/

Published by SOP3 Publishing
www.sop3publishing.com

Paperback ISBN: 978-0-9857690-4-8
Digital Edition ISBN: 978-0-9857690-5-5
Library of Congress Control Number: 2016908844

*This book is dedicated to the people on the front lines committed to helping save animals' lives—whether working or volunteering directly in a shelter, with a rescue organization or in any other capacity. Your efforts are meaningful and make a difference.*

# CONTENTS

# ABOUT THIS BOOK

*"Until one loves an animal, part of one's soul remains unawakened."*
—Anatole France

## "CAN WE GET A DOG, PLEASE?"

This probably sounds familiar to you, whether it's coming from your children, your partner or your own inner voice. If you, or anyone you know is even considering adopting a dog, you are holding the perfect guide to help make the process easy.

Over the years I have received numerous calls from friends and acquaintances with questions about dogs and dog adoption. Many people think adopting a dog can be "risky." They don't know where to begin and want to make sure they find the perfect dog for their family. I'm always happy to spend time on the phone offering guidance. I wrote *What to Expect When Adopting a Dog* as if I was helping *you* out over the phone.

*What to Expect When Adopting a Dog* provides the basic information you need to choose and care for your new family member in an easy-to-read, digestible format. It includes helpful anecdotes from experienced dog parents and pet professionals as well as a compilation of the best articles on the Internet about animal care for you to easily reference. All of the pet professionals who have contributed to this book are happy to share their expertise further with you, so feel free to contact them to learn more.

I share many tips I've learned from personal experience, having parented several wonderful rescued dogs over the past 20 years. Admittedly my pet parenting wasn't always perfect, but you can avoid the fumbles I experienced by reading *What to Expect When Adopting a Dog.* I also share my expertise as a former board member of a small rescue organization, a Certified Humane Education Specialist through Humane Society University, as a pet adoption center volunteer and as an author of humane education books.

Don't be the person who says, "If I had just known that little bit of information, the whole process would have been so much easier." Even if you are just considering adopting a dog, this book will inform you about the adoption process as well as the lifetime care of your dog, so you can be prepared when the time is right.

The information is broken up into modules so you can easily reference any given topic as necessary. For even more detailed information, open the links to the articles and stories in each module to delve deeper. *What To Expect When Adopting a Dog* offers you convenient answers to the most-asked questions.

*"My friends just rescued two puppies and they didn't know where to begin. Thank you, Diane, for all the tips and resources and pointing everyone in the right direction."*
—Lisa Hacken,
Happy Dog Parent to Reuben, the 103 lb. Adopted Mutt

*"We rescued the most handsome big mush of a Boxer on Saturday. Thanks again, Diane, for chatting with me, and sharing your knowledge about the process. I really appreciate it!"*
—Melissa and Mars Sandoval,
Proud Dog Parents of Dino, the Rescued Boxer

*"Our son Dylan was terrified of dogs and wouldn't go over to friends' houses who had dogs. Our daughter, Aidan, however, was asking for a dog. We figured that if we were going to do this we wanted a small, calm breed that didn't shed a lot, and we were prepared to go to a breeder. After speaking with Diane, we (reluctantly) agreed to consider adopting a dog from a rescue and were able to find a local, breed-specific rescue organization. We didn't get the exact breed we thought we wanted, but we all fell in love with Cleo and can't imagine life without her."*

—Natalie and Max Stone,
Dog Parents to Cleo, the Mixed Breed Rescued Dog

The human bond with dogs dates back thousands of years if not farther and today there are countless organizations promoting the myriad ways dogs help humans and humans help dogs. Dogs enrich our lives immeasurably, from improving our physical and psychological health to inspiring compassion and responsibility in our children. They affect us profoundly as they become an integral part of the family. This is why we must learn to care for them in the best way we can and treat them like beloved family members. In return, we receive unconditional love, a confidant, a constant companion, enthusiastic greetings at the door and a whole lot of entertainment.

# INTRODUCTION

TWENTY YEARS AGO, MY HUSBAND and I had big plans to buy a Golden Retriever from a dog breeder. We had just begun researching nearby breeders when we got a call from our friend, Chris. He told us he had found a stray puppy sniffing around a garbage can at the neighborhood soccer field, wearing a choke collar that was too tight. Chris knew about our plans to purchase a new dog and called to see if we would take this puppy instead, since dogs weren't allowed in his small apartment. My heart sank at the thought of getting stuck with a mangy stray instead of having the chance to choose a perfect new Golden Retriever. You should have seen my body language. Arms crossed I grumbled, "We can look at him, but that's it. We're just looking." I was set on buying my Golden Retriever.

To my surprise and delight, I took one look at this puppy and fell in love. He wasn't at all what I expected. His cute floppy ears, sweet brown eyes and wagging tail melted my heart—it was love at first sight, despite his desperate need for a bath. My husband and I placed signs in the neighborhood and checked with the local shelter to make sure no one was looking for this neglected puppy. We soon realized he was ours to protect and love and we named him JJ. Little did we know what an impact JJ would have on our lives.

After rescuing JJ, I learned about the millions of homeless animals being euthanized every year and became passionate about promoting awareness of animal abuse, neglect and overpopulation. Thus began my journey.

For the record, I still think Golden Retrievers are absolutely gorgeous, but during my journey I learned that it's not the breed or size or shape of the dog that makes him loveable. Rather, as I've grown fond of saying, it's the "dogness" of the dog. They don't need any special papers or specific lineage to offer the unconditional love that only a dog can.

Here's how *What to Expect When Adopting a Dog* is laid out:

**Module 1**: Taking the First Steps

In the first module, I help you determine whether you are ready to take on the responsibility of a new dog. Your answers to the "Am I Ready?" quizzes will get you thinking about the time, energy and resources involved. Then we consider characteristics that may be important to you.

**Module 2**: Ok, You're Ready. What Now?

In the second module, I provide information on shelters, rescue organizations and Internet resources to help you find your perfect pup. However you choose to bring a dog into your life, my highest wish is for you to know the unconditional love they offer. I personally advocate for adoption over breeders or pet stores, which is discussed in-depth in Module 2.

**Module 3**: Preparing Your Home

In the third module, you learn what you should have on hand before your dog arrives and about basic care. From supplies to vet visits, I help you feel prepared.

**Module 4**: Integrating Your Dog into Your Home

In Module 4 you will learn about introducing your new dog to your family members, furry and human alike, as well as getting them acquainted with your surroundings. There is safety information for the whole family, as well as must-have tips on basic training, exercise and socialization.

**Module 5**: Advanced Dog Parenting

In the fifth module, you are introduced to a plethora of resources to keep you and your pet engaged, well exercised, comfortable and happy for years to come.

**How to read this book**: *What to Expect When Adopting a Dog* contains more than 100 links to blogs and articles, along with some recommended products. They are optional of course but available for you to read more in-depth about certain topics. If you are reading the electronic version you can click directly on the links for more information. Since you are reading the paper version, you can instead refer to the link library at www.dianerosesolomon.com/links. Hyperlinks are indicated using a $^\Delta$ symbol. Links to every article, website and organization can be found on my website or listed in the back of the book.

Additionally, I use the pronoun "he" referring to dogs throughout the book for convenience and consistency though of course not all dogs are male.

Dogs are pretty amazing. They don't care where you live, your financial or marital status or what you look like. They want to give and receive love. Pretty basic. It is really quite magical. Enjoy the journey!

# MODULE 1

# TAKING THE FIRST STEPS

*"When the Man waked up he said, 'What is Wild Dog doing here?'*
*And the Woman said 'his name is not Wild Dog anymore, but the*
*First Friend, because he will be our friend for always and always*
*and always.'"*

—Rudyard Kipling

## PART I

## AM I READY?

ADOPTING A DOG MEANS COMMITTING yourself to the lifelong care of a dog who for some reason has found himself homeless. The process is often facilitated by shelters and rescue organizations, which provide temporary homes for stray and relinquished dogs. The term dog adoption, in this book, and commonly in the animal rescue world, does not apply when they are purchased from a breeder.

Many dogs can also be found living in the streets and in some areas of the US and abroad, street dogs are all too common. Perhaps you've witnessed a dog in the streets and wondered if they have just escaped from a loving home or are homeless and in need of assistance.

Every homeless dog has a story. Due to countless unfortunate reasons, thousands of perfectly adoptable dogs have ended up in the shelter. Some have endured hideous abuse and neglect. Others have been left behind in a move or abandoned for financial reasons. The list goes on. Whatever his story, every dog deserves a stable, loving, "forever home" so he needn't ever return to a shelter.

Adopting a dog is extremely fun and rewarding, but it is also a big responsibility. Before adopting a dog, you must understand that you will be dedicating considerable time and finances to his care and comfort. It is essential that you commit to training, regular exercise, veterinary care, the highest quality food you can afford and as much patience as you can muster.

In this module, I help you determine whether you are ready for this responsibility, and get clarity on some important resources you will need.

It is important that the whole family be involved in the adoption and care of your dog. Whether you are single, attached, married with kids or without, you *are* a family once you have a dog! So this book applies to your arrangement however it looks. If you're just embarking on the dog-parenting journey you are about to experience how much happiness they bring to your life. Adopting a dog strengthens the family bond even before he arrives. Together you have taken on a long-term responsibility to be good caretakers to a dog in need for his entire life.

Each family member develops his or her own special relationship with the dog including age-appropriate responsibilities. I have witnessed families where one member was reluctant to adopt a new dog and ended up falling in love anyway. But it is prudent for everyone to be on board.

Before you embark on the dog-parenting journey, here are a few basic questions you should ask yourself:

**Do I have the time/energy?**

1. Am I willing and able to feed and water my dog daily?
2. Am I willing to take my dog on regular walks and spend time exercising and playing with him?
3. Will my new dog affect the way I am able to care for pets I already have?
4. Does everyone living in my house agree on the decision to add a dog to the family?
5. Am I willing to put in the effort to be patient and diligent during the chewing and housebreaking stages? (Protecting your things without getting overly frustrated.)
6. Am I willing to train my dog?
7. Is anyone in my family allergic to dogs?
8. Will there be a new baby in the house any time soon?
9. Am I open to falling in love with my dog and caring for him until the end of his life?

## Do I have the resources?

1. Does my apartment or house rental allow pets?
2. Am I willing and able to spay or neuter and microchip my dog?
3. Am I prepared to take my dog to the vet for annual check-ups and emergencies and pay for all of his recommended vaccinations and care?
4. Is there someone to care for my dog when I'm not around or traveling? Am I willing to hire a dog-walker or enroll him in professional daycare if my dog will be alone for extended periods of time?
5. Is my house/yard big enough for the breed I want?
6. Can I afford quality pet food, toys, and treats and pet care when I travel?
7. Can I accommodate my dog if he travels with me?

*"Building a relationship with a pet is like building any other relationship in your life. It takes time, commitment, observation, patience and love. You have to be someone your pet can count on—always."*
—Jeannette Hartman, Fido Universe
www.fidouniverse.com

While it is generally less expensive to adopt than purchasing from a breeder, it is critical to enter this relationship knowing the true financial costs of pet care.

Carolyn Shadle, PH.D. (www.VeterinarianCommunication.com) conveys the importance of having a relationship with a trusted veterinarian so that costs are understood, one of many important points she outlined in the June 2015 issue of TRENDS Magazine, published by The American Animal Hospital Association (AAHA) for the professional veterinary community.

The American Veterinary Medical Association (AVMA™) shares tips to understand veterinary costs, suggestions for preventive care, and financial assistance. An excerpt from an article on their website reminds us… "But emergencies, injuries and illnesses can happen, and they can be associated with higher costs for diagnosis and treatment. Ideally, pet owners should plan for these expenses and set aside money to cover them."Δ

The American Society for the Prevention of Cruelty to Animals® (ASPCA® ) offers a table with projected annual costs for different sized dogs which can be found in the link library.Δ

The good news is that there are wellness programs and pet insurance that you can purchase to help mitigate veterinary costs. (More about pet insurance in Module 5.) The even better news is that a study was just released by the Human Animal Bond Research Initiative (HABRI)Δ showing that pet ownership saves an estimated $11.7 billion in human health care costs.

While I maintain that a family should be comfortable with the financial responsibilities of pet parenting, the benefits, including the potential financial benefits due to improved overall health are now documented.

> Remember that dogs are not a good surprise gift. People often want to participate in the choosing process and a surprise dog might not come at the right time for the recipient which doesn't set up the relationship for success.

---

ΔThis is the first occurrence where a link is indicated using the Δ symbol. Throughout this book, any time a section of text contains this symbol it means there is a corresponding link with more detailed information at dianerosesolomon.com/links

# BEGINNING THE SEARCH

IF YOU FEEL GOOD ABOUT your answers to the questionnaire, you are ready to begin the search for your perfect family dog. Be aware that different types of dogs require different levels of care and choosing the right one for you and your family is the first step in setting up a successful pet/parent relationship. This decision should be based on a multitude of factors, including age, size, breed and temperament.

## Age

**Puppies**:

Is that cute puppy the best choice for your lifestyle, or might you be better matched with a mature, calmer dog? The wonderful thing about puppies is that you have the opportunity to socialize them properly from a young age. You get to watch them grow from silly fluff balls into loveable family members. But remember that even though puppies are a lot of fun, they are also a ton of work.

*"When we arrived at the house with the puppies, they were spilling out all over from a plastic baby swimming pool that could barely contain the 10 tumbling and tangled little bodies—I didn't know how to pick. Having criteria prior to picking out a pup seems smart, but you'll find it's a matter of heart because the head has temporar-*

*ily left the body. There was one big, hunky male sitting alone as all the other pups clamored for attention—he was a bit comical and watching me. Somehow I knew and I think somehow you will too. If you don't feel a pull on your heart and a pit in your gut, better to not get a puppy because when you have one you'll find they are closer to you than skin and infiltrate your life in ways you didn't imagine and can't live without. We named him Earl and even though you couldn't see them, I'm pretty certain he had angel wings."*

—Shawna Schuh, President,
Women in the Pet Industry Network
www.womeninthepetindustry.com

This gut feeling Shawna mentions applies to adult dogs as well. I didn't want a puppy when we went to find the last two dogs we adopted, because I knew how much attention and effort is required. Despite my concern about the additional responsibility of taking care of a puppy, my family got their way when we found 6-month-old Gonzo at the rescue organization. Once he was in our home I fell in love and committed to him even though it was extra work for me.

It is not uncommon for the whole family to want a puppy; yet one of the adults ends up being the primary caretaker no matter how much everyone promises they will help. Know your limitations in advance. I was a sucker but it worked out.

Most shelters and rescue organizations run adoptions on a first come, first served basis (assuming the families applying are all good candidates). Puppies are popular and multiple people often want the same pup at the shelter. Our local shelter holds an auction for puppies. Two friends of mine recently found super cute puppies at an auc-

Ninja is a black dog, which can be another strike against shelter dogs. Black Dog Syndrome is thought of as a random fear of black dogs that makes it difficult for them to find homes. It is similar to the black cat superstition. It's also harder to get a good photo of a black dog, making them more difficult to showcase. Some organizations host special adoption days for black dogs at discounted prices to help get them extra attention. While it appears black dogs do languish longer in shelters, I recently learned that there are also more black dogs entering the shelters, so perhaps Black Dog Syndrome is more myth than previously considered. Ultimately there are many factors and you should choose the dog whose heart calls to yours.

tion where there were enough puppies for everyone who showed up.

For a comprehensive guide on puppyhood, you can download Adopt-a-pet.com's FREE puppy manual.△

**Adult Dogs**:

People often assume adult dogs in the shelter are damaged, or they just want a cute puppy and potentially wonderful dogs are often overlooked.

Most adult dogs are already house broken and don't require the same level of diligence, constant feeding and potty training that puppies require. They are already full sized so you know how big they are going to be. Many adult dogs still have plenty of pep in their step if you're looking for a companion to match your active lifestyle.

The next time we were ready for a dog, we all agreed on an adult dog and adopted Ninja when he was two years old. I didn't have time for the extra work a puppy requires, and I knew that adult dogs often have a hard time finding homes.

You could also consider opening your heart to a senior or special needs dog. There is a whole spectrum of what a special need is. You may fall in love with a dog despite or because of that special need. (More about senior and special needs dogs in Module 5.)

My stepbrother and sister-in-law wanted an adult dog and fell in love with a Shih Tzu. It wasn't until after they signed the adoption papers that they learned he was at least 12!

## Size

Size matters as well. Think about your lifestyle and hobbies and how you will incorporate your dog. If you want a small dog who can travel under your seat on an airplane, then a Mastiff obviously isn't the best choice. Walking my strong Labrador/Pit Bull mix is challenging and not for someone anticipating a small cuddly dog. Caring for big dogs can be more expensive as they eat more and often cost more to groom. Additionally, apartment buildings may allow dogs but restrict size (or breed! Please read information below about Breed Specific Legislation).

## Breed

Every breed has "typical" traits and behaviors. It just takes a little research to determine which breeds have the traits best suited to your family. For example, Welsh Corgis are generally smart, easy to train and loyal, but they are also known to bark and nip. Greyhounds are calm and polite, but can also be fearful and timid.

Here's more insight into some other breed issues.

*"[At Sweetwater Valley Dog Rescue] I mostly deal with larger dogs... many hounds including Catahoulas. When people inquire about the breed, I ask them if they know much about the activity requirements of this breed. And if they say 'no, we were planning on keeping him in the crate a lot,' I have to turn them away. While no dog belongs in a crate all day (Would YOU want to be stuck in a crate all day?) this breed, and many others like it, requires exercise, stimulation and a 'job'."*

—Steve M. Hamm, Sweetwater Valley Dog Rescue
https://www.sweetwatervalleyrescue.com/

Despite the growing popularity of poodle mixes (Labradoodles, Goldendoodles, Cockapoos, Maltipoos, etc.) buyer beware! Some families purchase Labradoodles for example, in search of a hypoallergenic dog with a Labrador (ideally calm) personality and instead get a dog who is high strung and not great with kids. Many designer dogs like these are being relinquished to the shelters because the expectations of that "perfect dog" aren't met. The fact that there are Doodle rescue organizations that have rescued thousands of Doodles speaks volumes. One of my favorite dogs in the neighborhood is a Golden Doodle and he is awesome. But it is important to be informed.

If you are looking for a hypoallergenic dog,[Δ] Adopt-a-Pet.com offers information about "low dander" dogs as well as tips to help reduce allergies.[Δ]

On the flip side, there is also a gross misconception that "Pit Bulls" and other "bully" dog breeds are dangerous. "Pit Bull" is *not* actually a breed. According to Modern Dog Magazine.com, *"'Pit Bull' is, in fact, a loose term for many distinct "bully" breed dogs, such as the American*

*Staffordshire Terrier, the American Pit Bull Terrier, and the Staffordshire Bull Terrier."*

Despite the often-maligned stereotype, many resources confirm what intelligent, loving, loyal creatures Pit Bulls truly are.

> *"According to testing by The National Canine Temperament Testing Association, the Golden Retriever, Poodle, Border Collie, English Setter and numerous other breeds are considered more likely to become aggressive than the breeds commonly referred to as Pit Bulls. While the average score of the 231 breeds tested was a mere 82.4 percent, Pit Bulls scored a 86.5 percent (the higher the score the better)."*
>
> —Modern Dog Magazine
> www.moderndogmagazine.com

Read the full article, "What is it About Pit Bulls?"[Δ] from ModernDogMagazine.com.

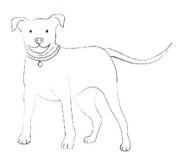

As a Pit Bull mix dog parent I can truly attest to their sweetness. Being a Pit Bull parent requires a certain amount of diligence that other breeds might not require due to their reputation and strength. But Pitties have offered us as much love, amusement and companionship as any other dog we've parented.

Having a breed that usually doesn't bite does not mean your dog will never bite anyone. No matter which breed you choose, you should always consult a professional trainer or behaviorist if your pet is exhibiting any aggressive or dangerous behavior.

*"It's about the individual dog personality and the chemistry you feel together (yep, we have chemistry with animals just like we do with other humans!). And don't forget about those marvelous mutts! Not only do you get a one-of-a-kind companion, but many veterinarians say that mixed-breed dogs tend to be healthier than purebred dogs, who tend to be prone to certain genetic conditions, depending on the breed."*
—Adopt-a-Pet.com

Another consideration when choosing a dog is to find out if there are there Breed Specific Legislation laws in your town prohibiting the adoption of the breed you are interested in. Breed Specific Legislation (BSL) is defined as a law or statute that equates the qualities of a dangerous dog with a certain breed, and bans or restricts certain breeds based on identity, not behavior of a specific animal. Please read more from the Animal Legal and Historical Center about BSL.[△]

For more about specific breeds please visit Adopt-a-pet.com's dog breed selector.[△]

## Temperament

Dogs, like people, vary in temperament. Some are sweet and cuddly, while others are energetic or standoffish. If you want a hiking companion that can keep up with you, then a high-energy dog is a good fit. If you just want a buddy to snuggle up with when you get home at the end of the day, then a lower-energy dog may be best.

Ultimately there's no guarantee that any one breed will satisfy all of your requirements, but in all likelihood, you will fall in love with whichever dog you choose and any perceived shortcomings will fade away. Sometimes you just meet your perfect dog and you know instantly.

*"OOh- look at this guy. I think I'm in love."*

Luckily our first dog JJ had a gentle temperament. I don't know how I would have handled the more challenging dogs I have now if we had adopted them first. JJ was a good "starter" dog who helped me hone my skills as a dog parent so I could go on to manage stronger and feistier dogs. We believe JJ was a mix of a Sheltie (Shetland Sheepdog), some other kind of Shepherd and possibly a Labrador. It didn't occur to us that Shelties were herding breeds until we had kids and he would nip at their heels. He thought they were sheep! Other than that, he was very sweet natured and a great family dog. (More about dogs and kid safety in Module 4.)

Do you have an idea of the kind of dog you would like to add to your family? Or are you open to the dog that steals your heart? I'd love to hear how your search begins!

**A note on adopting a second dog:**

Perhaps you already have a dog and are thinking about adopting another. Great idea (assuming everyone is on board)! Two dogs are better than one. It's important, though, to be respectful of your current dog's temperament. Adding a new dog to the family can be a stressful experience for your current dog. Please see Module 4 for more tips to ease the transition.

The final, most important question is: Are you are ready to offer a dog a forever home and accept the unconditional love he has to offer? If so, read on!

# MODULE 2

# OK, YOU'RE READY.
# WHAT NOW?

*"I think dogs are the most amazing creatures; they give uncondi-
tional love. For me, they are the role models for being alive."*
—Gilda Radner

## PART I

## WHERE DO I GO TO ADOPT A DOG?

CONGRATULATIONS, YOU ARE READY TO BEGIN the adoption
process! In Module 2, I take you step-by-step through the process of
finding an adoptable dog in your area. I show you what to expect at a
shelter or rescue organization and provide a list of questions you may
be asked as a potential pet parent as well as the questions *you* should ask
the shelter or rescue group about your prospective pup. I also show you
how easy searching online for an adoptable dog can be.

Let's explore some of the ways you can go about finding your perfect dog.

1. Animal Shelter
2. Rescue Organization
3. Fostering
4. Online Adoption Resource

Some people just want to meet their potential dog in person and fall in love at first sight. If that sounds like you, go straight to your local shelter or rescue organization.

**What is the difference between a rescue organization and a shelter?**

## Animal Shelters

Shelters provide a temporary home for abandoned or homeless animals. They can be publically or privately managed. Most have limited space and must euthanize animals to make room for new ones, but some "no kill" and even "low kill" shelters do exist.

For a detailed explanation of the differences between "kill", "no kill" and "low kill" shelters, please visit an article that appears on Pet360.com.△

Some people adopt from the city or county animal shelter where there are hundreds of dogs to choose from, many of whom have been living there for a while and some who only have days or hours left before they are scheduled to be euthanized. Either way these dogs desperately need homes.

While shelter conditions range from squalid to rather decent, they are consistently loud and stressful environments. Many dogs become depressed or anxious from the stress and don't show their best selves when visitors come by their kennels. Even though the shelter environment may not be ideal, all it takes is one special look from a certain pooch and you know they are yours.

*"Our family was ready for a new dog. My heart told me to go to the shelter but many of my friends told me it was a bad idea. I'm so glad I ultimately followed my instinct to go get that puppy at the shelter because Parker is awesome and deserves a home just as much as a puppy from a breeder."*
—Daniel and Griselda Mayorga,
Proud Dog Parents to Parker, the Shelter Pup

Not only could you be saving a dog who is "red-listed" to be euthanized at the shelter, but most shelters allow you to adopt a dog the same day that you choose him, making the process of saving a life simple.

## Rescue Organizations

For some dogs, local rescue groups are their best chance at adoption. (Note that the term rescue in this book refers to dogs whose lives are rescued from euthanasia or abuse, not to search and rescue dogs.) Some rescue groups specialize in specific breeds or special needs dogs and you can serach for breed rescues online (see below).

Other rescue groups take in breeds or a specific sized dog to accommodate a geographic need. For example, there are countless Chihuahuas in California. Both major and private airlines assist in airlifting Chihuahuas to the East Coast where people in search of small dogs are waiting to adopt them. Similarly, the dog overpopulation problem is egregious in the South, yet there are amazing rescue groups transporting many to families waiting for them through rescue group partnerships in other states.

Some rescue groups visit local shelters and "rescue" the dogs they believe are adoptable and either board them or find fosters to take care of them while they await their forever homes. Most rescue organizations hold local adoption events where you can go and meet their dogs and many of them post information online about their dogs as well.

Whether the dog is living with a foster family or in a boarding facility, the rescue organization is able to gain information about his nature and tendencies, which is helpful for any potential adopter. In order for these organizations to ensure their dogs are going to good homes, you first submit a written application and then many require a home visit from a representative once your application has been approved.

*"Here are three bits of advice about searching for your newest family member.*

*First, if you are interested in a certain breed, research the breed and make sure you know what you are getting yourself into. Have a sense of that breed's temperament, common medical issues (and associated costs) exercise needs, etc.*

*Second, remember the cutest may not be the best fit for your family and lifestyle. A good rescue organization can help match you with the best dog for you.*

*Last and possibly the most important, remember that this dog has lost his forever home. Perhaps he was passed from person to person, or locked in a cage, or dumped on the street and he certainly does not understand why. So, when you bring him home give him time to trust and love you. You will have a loyal companion offering you endless joy for years."*

—Mona Straub, "Official Matchmaker",
Dachshund Rescue South Florida and Founder, Just Fur Fun
www.justfurfunonline.com

## Where do I find shelters and adoption events?

The easiest way to visit a shelter is to check their hours online and drop in. It's easier to reach a live person on the phone when contacting a smaller shelter, but it's often difficult to reach anyone to plan an in-person visit at a larger shelter. If you have questions about a dog at a city shelter, the best thing to do is show up in person to see him. Many animals have limited time, so if your forever dog is living at a high kill shelter, your timing could be perfect.

If you know the name of a rescue group and wish to visit one of their adoption days, check their website for a schedule of events. Additionally, you can find a local shelter or the many adoption events in your area by going to a networked pet database, such as Petfinder.com or Adopt-a-pet.com (more about them below).

*"Three of my dogs passed in a two-year period and I was devastated. I never thought I'd be able to open my heart again. Months later, I saw a flyer for a Best Friends Adoption Fair and pondered going just to be around dogs. The night before the event, I had a dream. My three dogs were together and said, 'Mom, go. And go to the far back corner on the right.' The dream was so vivid I couldn't shake it. The next day, I went to the fair and there, in the far back corner on the right, I saw a very thin, frightened, tall black dog. She caught my eye with a look that was so penetrating—I knew she was the one I was meant to find. My beautiful Grace has been with me ever since."*
—Beth Larsen, Founder, Waggletops®
www.waggletops.com

Best Friends Animal Society△ is on the forefront of the No Kill movement. Best Friends is headquartered in in Kanab, Utah, where they operate the nation's largest no-kill companion animal sanctuary. Best Friends Animal Sanctuary is home to about 1,700 animals, many of whom just need a second chance or have special needs and require extra attention. Their mission is "No More Homeless Pets." Through organizing and facilitating massive adoption events, and spay and neuter and educational programs, they are leading the way to a No Kill society. Best Friends recently established two adoption centers in Los Angeles, one in Salt Lake City (and as of this edition will also be opening a center in New York City in 2016). By working with the shelters and local rescue organizations, they are making a big difference in reducing the number of animals euthanized. Their ambitious plan is for LA to be a No Kill city by 2017.

For more information about Best Friends Animal Society and their coalition, please visit Best Friends.[Δ]

*"We've always loved our two rescue pets, but we weren't really looking for a new family member. Then we saw Lulu, a little Bull Terrier at a No-Kill LA (NKLA) event last November. There was just this immediate connection with her gentle soulfulness. She was 'the best dog Angel City Pits had ever rescued', according to the volunteer who had fostered her, so we took the plunge and left the event with a dog we never intended to rescue and she brings us joy every day. I want to stress that all dogs aren't alike. Hang out with a lot of dogs before choosing the being to which you will pledge a lifetime of care and love. Follow your heart. You won't be disappointed!"*
—Arthur Jeon and Leah Lessard, Global Animal
www.globalanimal.org

## Fostering

If you're not ready to commit to adoption, but you still want to help a dog in need, fostering is a great option. Fostering through a rescue organization means having a dog come live with you until the organization finds him a forever home. Many of these organizations completely rely on foster families, as they have no facility to board the dogs they rescue. These organizations identify adoptable dogs in the shelter and place them into foster homes. Then they post photos and a description about the pups online on their website and/or perhaps on Adopt-a-pet.com or Petfinder.com.

Some organizations will help pay for the dog's care, which is good news for people who really want to adopt but can't currently afford a dog of their own. Sometimes, though it is the foster family's obligation to pay for food, vet bills, etc. so you will need to inquire before committing. Your job will be to love and care for the dog as if he were your own while bringing him to adoption events where he can potentially meet his forever family face to face. Oftentimes people start out fostering a dog then end up falling in love and adopting him. That is affectionately called a "foster failure" and is a true success.

The huge advantage for a dog being fostered is that they are living in a home environment, getting socialized, and sometimes living with other pets and kids. Some families who already have a dog choose to foster because they want to help out as many dogs as they can, not just the ones they've adopted.

My friends, Katrina and Jim, already had a dog and thought they might test the waters of parenting a second dog by fostering. They figured by fostering they'd get a pretty good idea if they were ready, plus the bonus of helping an animal in need.

They learned about New York-based Pet Rescue$^\Delta$ group that mostly receives dogs transported from southern states who are rescued from high kill shelters. From there they find people willing to foster them.

Katrina and Jim connected with a one-year-old dog and then…

*"Pet Rescue insisted on meeting all members of the family (including our dog Peanut) and anyone else who would be interacting with the new dog (the dog walker, a nanny or housekeeper if we had one) to ensure that everyone was on board and that the foster dog would be a good match for our family dynamic, work schedules and activity levels.*

*Because of the careful screening and meticulous pairing by Pet Rescue, our first foster dog perfectly complemented our current dog's demeanor. We named him Yogi and quickly realized that he fit in perfectly and now Yogi is a permanent member of our family. Yogi is a perfect example of a 'foster failure'!"*

—Katrina and Jim Cantwell,
Proud Dog Parents to Peanut and Yogi

Find out more from Petfinder.com△ about what it entails to foster a dog, and how to prepare your home for fostering.

Katrina shared with me the importance of fostering as a means of acclimating street dogs to living in a home, whether the foster family ends up adopting (like she did) or the foster leads to adoption by another qualified family.

## What about searching online? What are my options?

Two wonderful resources, Petfinder.com and Adopt-a-pet.com can make your search super easy. They are well-organized databases that allow you to search through thousands of pet bios and customize your search by location, breed, age, size, rescue organization and more. It's as easy as clicking a few tabs and within seconds more dogs than you could possibly visit in a week appear before your eyes. For example, if you are looking to adopt a young female Yorkie within 50 miles, you can narrow your search to be that specific. Many of the descriptions give you detailed information about the dog's temperament and needs, as well as photos and videos. Pay close attention to this information. Sometimes the pet you want is available right away, other times you may be put on a waiting list for a specific breed/age. (Adopt-a-pet.com has a great notification feature for waiting lists.) You may find that your perfect pet is a mixed version of the breed you wanted, or a little older or younger!

Your perfect pet might be in the town right next door! We found our most recent dog, Ninja, on Petfinder.com. I was mourning the loss of our dog T-bone and didn't have the energy to go to the shelter, so we narrowed down our choices through the database instead. It made the process very easy for my family. We saw a video of Ninja playing with his buddies and our family fell in love! Even though the boarding facility where he was living was pretty far away, we got lucky and one of the rescue group volunteers offered to bring him to us. We were able to introduce him to our dog Gonzo on neutral territory and went for a walk to see if they would be ok together. Once they seemed comfortable with one another, we brought them to my backyard to run around. They loved each other immediately and within a few weeks, it was as if Ninja had been here all along.

*"Mom- here's that website with all the dogs for adoption."*

## What do I do if I find a dog in the street?

When you come across a stray dog you should always use your best judgment before approaching him. He may be friendly and approachable, or he may be fearful or injured and possibly aggressive as a result. When in doubt, call your local animal control to help catch a dog running in the streets. They will scan his microchip if he has one and attempt to find his owner. If he does not have proper identification, he will remain at the local shelter, where the owner can attempt to find him. You can follow up to make sure he's found a good home, especially if your local shelter isn't a no kill facility. If he seems friendly and will come to you, check his tags to make sure he is not just an escapee. You can try bringing him to his home or calling the number on the tags to find his owner.

*"Last week I found a dog running in my neighborhood and didn't know what to do. We called Diane for advice after calling the number on the tag and not hearing back from anyone. She suggested we take the dog to the local shelter where they could scan her microchip, plus if anyone was looking for her, that's where they'd go. We wrote down the number the dog was assigned at the shelter and planned to make sure she was claimed.*

*Well the story has a happy ending because she was reunited with her very grateful family 30 minutes after we dropped her off. They had tented their house for termites and in the melee she ran off. It would have saved a lot of heartache if the family had used a cell phone rather than the home line on her tag and if she had been microchipped. A happy ending nonetheless."*

—Faith Foss and TJ Mahar,
Dog Parents to Sparky and Teddy, the Rescued Dogs

If it feels safe and the dog does not have identification, take him home with you while you contact your local shelter and veterinarian (where he can get his microchip scanned) and place signs up in the area making sure he doesn't belong to someone else. Maybe you'll fall in love! There are so many legitimately homeless dogs and finding you could be kismet. If the dog is registered with companies like PetHub, the PetHub.com[Δ] database could help find his home. Finding Rover,[Δ] another cool tool, is a facial recognition app that helps recover lost dogs.

A friend found our first dog JJ on a soccer field and my husband found T-bone and his sister Maggie on the roadside years later. They were all flea and worm ridden and clearly neglected. When no one responded to our posts, signs and inquiries, they were ours and our friends took Maggie!

For more thorough information about finding stray dogs, visit Rachel Marie Sheppard's website My Kid Has Paws and read her fabulous blog post: *What Should You Do When You See a Stray Dog.*[Δ]

# WHAT TO EXPECT AT THE SHELTER/RESCUE ORGANIZATION ADOPTION EVENT

BEFORE YOU BEGIN YOUR SEARCH, prepare yourself for the possibility that you may not find your perfect dog on your first outing. All family members, especially children, need to understand that the chemistry has to be right. It is also possible you *will* meet your perfect dog on your first outing. Be sure to read Module 3 before you go so you are prepared if you do bring a new dog home. Module 4 offers some important safety tips, which apply here as well. Most importantly, children should always be supervised at the shelter or adoption event.

## How to Greet a Dog at a Shelter/Rescue Event

Dogs you meet at the shelter or at adoption events are sometimes anxious due to their circumstances. They are usually kenneled or in a crate, which makes them even more vulnerable. Many dogs appear aloof which could be a sign of stress or a lack of socialization. It is important to be sensitive to their situation.

Never stare into a dog's eyes, tap on his crate or make barking noises at him. You and anyone accompanying you should always approach a dog calmly so he does not feel threatened. It's a good idea to ask one of the shelter employees or volunteers about a particular dog you are interested in before approaching him, especially if you have children with you. I recommend a great article from Debbie Jacobs of Fearfuldogs.com<sup>Δ</sup> on how to approach new dogs.

When you visit a shelter or adoption event, be prepared to answer the many questions you have probably already asked yourself.

## Sample questions you may be asked:

- Who is the primary caretaker?
- Are you aware this is a lifelong (the pet's lifetime) commitment?
- Will someone in the family be home all day? If not, how long will he be alone? Will he be confined? If so, is it to a specific room in your home or a crate? Who will care for your dog while you are out of the home or away for extended periods?
- Do you have a fenced in yard?
  - \* Many rescue organizations will do an at-home visit to make sure your gates and fences will properly contain your dog.
- What will you do if you run into financial trouble and are no longer able to care for your dog?
- Are you adopting this dog for protection or companionship?
- Do you have any other pets?
- Do you have children?
- Where will the dog live? Sleep? Indoors or out?

An article found in Vetstreet.com called "Why 'outdoor dogs' are miserable"<sup>Δ</sup> beautifully explains why it's a bad idea to plan to adopt a dog only to leave him outside.

> If you have another dog at home, be sure to tell the adoption counselor about any quirks your dog has so he or she can help pair you with the perfect new dog.

Equally important are the questions you prepare to ask the shelter employees or rescue organization. Since they see his behavior every day, they may have a good idea of his temperament and whether he is right for your situation. You will want to know as much about your potential new family member as possible before bringing him home.

*"Be open to suggestions from the adoption counselor when picking out a dog at the shelter. They know the dogs the best and truly are "matchmakers." Sometimes the one you pick out at first is the right one, but you may be pleasantly surprised at who they pick out for you!"*

—Cara Schepps, Former Shelter Adoption Counselor

## Sample questions to ask the shelter/rescue organization:

- How old is the dog?
- Is he housebroken?
- Does he have any health challenges? If so, what type of medical care might be required?
- Is he up to date on shots?
- Has the dog been spayed or neutered? (Neutering is important since there are already more pets than good homes and you want to be a responsible pet owner.)
- Is he microchipped? (Most shelters and rescue organizations won't release a dog until they are neutered and microchipped.)

- Has he lived with a family before?
- Is he ok around children? Babies? This is important especially if you already have kids or plan to bring your dog around other children.
- How does he react to other dogs? Cats?
- Where is he used to sleeping?
- Is he crate trained?
- Does he walk well on a leash?
- Does he have any obedience training?
- What kind of food does he eat? How often?
- Does your organization offer any in-home training?
- If we take the dog home and it doesn't work out, can we bring him back? (NOTE: This does not mean you should commit to a dog only to change your mind once he has settled in. You are asking about worst case scenarios—a dog who doesn't get along with another pet, or shows aggression toward a child, or is more of an allergy trigger than anticipated, etc. You want to know if it is possible to bring the dog back to the rescue organization within a couple of weeks so they can continue to search for his forever home. Many rescue groups offer a couple of weeks of "getting acquainted" during which time you haven't officially adopted the dog. They also may require that if you do have a problem and need to rehome your dog down the road you contact them first.)

Ultimately, you have many choices when it comes to finding your perfect dog to adopt, whether he comes from a shelter, rescue group or online resource. Depending on how far you cast your net, there are hundreds or thousands of dogs in all shapes, sizes, ages and breeds to choose from.

*"When I was searching for my current dog, I was committed to a rescue dog. I did have some general parameters: I live in a condo so I wanted a relatively small dog. I didn't want a 'yapper.' I didn't want a nervous or fragile dog. I didn't want a high maintenance dog that was going to require a lot of grooming. The general parameters were much more helpful than anything breed related."*

—Jeannette Hartman, Fido Universe

www.fidouniverse.com

# DOG ADOPTION VS. DOG BREEDERS

PERHAPS YOU ARE STILL ON the fence about adopting. Maybe you can't decide if you want a "sure thing" from a breeder or if you are willing to take a chance on a rescued pet. Here are some common misconceptions about buying vs. adopting.

## Myth #1

- "Rescued dogs can end up being more expensive overall."
  * While you may adopt a dog who needs some immediate training, or a special needs dog requiring accommodations, adopting a pet is generally less expensive than purchasing one. Adoption fees vary (usually in the $250-300 range, but they can be higher or lower) and sometimes fees are even waived at adoption fairs. The money you spend adopting a dog is used to defray expenses and create cash flow for the next pet to be saved. Your willingness to pay the fee indicates your willingness to spend money on your new family member now and as necessary for the life of the pet.
  * Many shelter dogs are mixed breeds and are often healthier and have fewer genetic defects.
  * Further, there are irresponsible breeders who don't screen for common purebred ailments, which could potentially

lead to expensive veterinary bills. And it is common for the inbreeding in purebred dogs to cause other defects such as: a higher risk of cancer and tumors; eye and heart disease; joint and bone disorders; skin, immune system and neurological diseases; and even epilepsy: To learn more about purebred dog complications, please visit an article that originally appeared on petMD.com.△

* Countless purebred puppies originating from puppy mills come with serious health issues. Many have AKC designation, which offers information about their lineage, but doesn't protect them or their parents from the awfulness of the puppy mill. These puppies are usually sold in pet shops, at flea markets and online.

*"A puppy mill, sometimes known as a puppy farm, is a commercial dog breeding facility that is operated with an emphasis on profits above animal welfare. Breeding dogs often live in substandard conditions. They are forced to breed over and over again and typically are never let out of their cages and never feel grass beneath their feet or sunshine on their faces. Puppies are often sick upon arrival at pet shops and may have genetic defects that become apparent only after the contract with the pet shop expires. Please never buy puppies from pet shops or flea markets. There are so many options when it comes to adopting a dog. Shelters are a great place to start."*
—Reem Regina Tatar, Founder, puppymillawareness.com

Though many cities have banned the sale of puppies in pet stores, there are still hundreds of pet stores thriving off of the impulse purchases of shoppers at the mall. I highly discourage purchases from any pet store. Many pet stores lie about obtaining their dogs from "reputable breeders," when they really get them from puppy mills.

Please note that many reputable pet stores DO hold pet adoption events through local rescue organizations. If the dogs there are dogs in need of homes, rather than puppies from a breeder or puppy mill, the rescue organization will be clearly identified. You can learn more about puppy mills from the ASPCA®.△

## Myth #2

- "You cannot find any specific breed at a shelter or rescue organization."
  - \* There are actually breed rescues for almost any breed of your choice. Petfinder.com and Adopt-a-pet.com make it easy to search for a specific breed.

*"When I was ready to adopt my first dog I had my heart set on a Golden Retriever. But finding one was going to be a challenge. I didn't want to go to a breeder, so I began researching rescue organizations online. I was thrilled when I discovered the Southern California Golden Retriever Rescue organization. They take in Golden Retrievers in need, providing them with veterinary care, rehabilitation and loving homes. I submitted an application, participated in an in-home interview and waited anxiously for my new dog. One month later I was matched up with a 4-year old Golden named Ally who had been rescued from a breeder. Without a doubt, it was one of the best decisions I ever made. She's given our family so much happiness and love."*

—Sam Bryant,
Dog Parent to Ally, the Rescued Purebred Golden Retriever

## Myth #3

- "Purebred dogs from a breeder are less likely to bite than shelter dogs."
    * Purebred dogs are just as likely to bite. The tendency to bite has less to do with the breed and more to do with environment or circumstance. They could be injured, ill, feeling threatened, chasing what they consider prey, playing too hard and accidentally hurt you, or a myriad of other reasons.
    * And sometimes a dog has a screw loose and there is no explanation at all. They show no prior evidence of being aggressive and then they just bite, or worse. It is uncommon, but it happens, which is why it is prudent to exercise caution with any dog, especially if they are new to you.
    * For more on the subject of nature vs. nurture, you can read "Dog Bite Fatalities: Breed or Human Problem"[Δ] that originally appeared on petMD.com. Nowhere in this article or anywhere else that I've read does there seem to be evidence of a higher incidence of dog bites from formerly homeless dogs than from dogs who were raised from puppyhood.

Years ago my mom had a very sweet Shih Tzu named Sadye. One day, my five-year-old daughter was chasing her around. I took my eye off them for a moment and my daughter thought it would be a good idea to follow the dog into her crate. The crate is a safe haven for dogs and when an intruder enters, there's nowhere to run and the fight or flight instinct kicks in. In this case, the dog bit my daughter. Sadye was trying to get away from her but we were neither reading her body language nor honoring her desire to feel safe. Fortunately it was just a warning bite and the dog was little. But we learned our lesson to always watch our kids around dogs and realized that even a well-socialized dog from a breeder is capable of biting. There are now incredible dog bite prevention and safety videos available to help your family avoid being bitten by a dog. See Module 4 for links and more information.

## Myth #4

- "Shelter dogs are damaged."
  - \* You might think a dog at a shelter or rescue organization is damaged. After all, why did someone discard him? Here are a few reasons why people relinquish their dogs to the shelter:
    - ☐ Dogs are given as gifts and the recipient wasn't ready for the responsibility.
    - ☐ A family believes they can't afford their dog or they are forced to move to an apartment that doesn't allow pets.
    - ☐ Lack of training
    - ☐ Lifestyle changes
    - ☐ Moving
    - ☐ Not able to devote enough time
    - ☐ They are a breeder dog and no longer valuable to the breeder.

It is heartening to know that organizations like Downtown Dog Rescue have partnered with the LA Shelters to offer alternatives to relinquishing their pet. The first Shelter Intervention Program[Δ] was launched in 2013 and provides families with resources to help keep their pets. If you or anyone you know is having a challenge and considering relinquishing their dog, check with your local shelter to see if they offer any similar program or resources. Other organizations like PAWS LA[Δ] endeavor to help seniors and people living with HIV/AIDS by providing assistance in caring for their companion animals. Check out their website for a resource listing as well as other PAWS organizations around the country.

While there are a multitude of reasons why dogs are relinquished to the shelter, some of them are simply shocking and speak volumes about the people and not necessarily the dog. I recently heard a story about a dog being returned to a rescue organization after six years living with a family. They claimed that he no longer fit their lifestyle. When they took him to the beach off leash, he would run off. When asked if they ever trained him, the answer the family gave was "no."

Granted, there are dogs with "issues," some of which land them in the shelter. However, these issues are often easily resolved with love, patience and training. It's important to consider the quirks your family is willing to tolerate. Many dogs are perfectly fine and simply need a chance to get out of the shelter.

## Respectable Breeders

Some people may still choose to purchase a pet from a breeder. While it is not my recommendation (because there are so many shelter dogs in need of a home), if you do, please be sure to research the breeder intensely. Make sure you can meet the dog where he lives to see his living condition for yourself before committing. Do not make any purchases over the internet or from ads in your local paper, as pets sold over the internet are often obtained illegally, from, for example, backyard breeders or puppy mills EVEN WHEN THEIR CLAIM IS THAT IT IS LEGITIMATE.

Many respectable breeders love and care for their dogs and will always find a good home for their dogs once they are no longer producing puppies. Then again, there are less scrupulous breeders who only view their dogs as potential income and drop them at the shelter (or worse) when they are no longer valuable. Any time you can keep a dog out of the shelter you are saving him a lot of stress and potentially his life.

Here's a story about a breeder dog who was loved by the breeder and able to be rehomed once she was done producing puppies, making a lot of people really happy.

*"My husband saw a Norwich Terrier on our honeymoon and since then has always wanted a Norwich Terrier puppy. Although I like to rescue dogs, there was a compromise needed.*

*And then the magic happened: I was at the vet with our King Charles Spaniel who was a breeder reject because his teeth weren't perfect although he was perfect to us.*

*I saw a lady in the waiting room with a dog in a crate and inquired, 'What kind of dog is that?' She opened the door and out popped a Norwich Terrier. She said, 'Meet Halle.' I said, 'Halle Halliday!' as I just knew one day that dog would be ours. It turns*

*out the woman was a breeder and this dog could be rehomed short-*
*ly after she had her last litter of puppies. Soon thereafter she retired*
*with us and is the best dog!"*

—Jeni Ellis Halliday, Founder, Halli-Loo™

Halli-loo.com

## The Importance of Dog Adoption

Ultimately, I can't stress enough how important it is to consider adoption. There isn't enough room in the shelters for all the animals and many perfectly healthy, adoptable pets are euthanized. According to the Humane Society of the United States (HSUS),[Δ] 6-8 million adoptable pets enter the shelter system each year. Of those, approximately half find homes and the rest are euthanized. You have the power to make a difference by choosing to adopt your next pet and encouraging friends and family to do the same.

By adopting a pet from a shelter or rescue organization you are saving a life and making room for another pet in that shelter. My experience shows that there is no difference between a dog adopted from a shelter and a dog purchased from a breeder other than the knowledge of the parents' lineage. Many purebred dogs from breeders or pet shops can come with behavioral or health issues.

Oftentimes there is limited information about a shelter dog's history. Maybe they were neglected or abused, but they deserve to be loved and cared for as much as any other dog. With patience and training, almost any dog is capable of settling in and being a loyal companion.

*"I can tell you why people WANT to adopt rescue dogs. It feels great*
*saving a life and knowing you made a difference for someone else*
*when you are in a position to do so. Dogs know when they have*
*been saved and you can see how grateful they are every day. There*

*are lots of purebreds who need a home, so if that's your thing then it's not a problem. Mixed breed dogs often have fewer health issues and are smarter and easier. It also costs less to rescue a dog than buy one from a breeder. You have a great conversation piece where you can talk about how he/she came to be with you and the fun little dimensions you get to discover in this sweet little creature that has become your best friend."*

—Candace Modrell, Director of Transports,
Shelter Transport Animal Rescue Team (S.T.A.R.T)
www.startrescue.org

Now that you are on your way to finding your perfect pup, be sure to read Module 3 to find out what you will need to be prepared when he first comes home.

Where did you search for your dog? Did your dog find you? I'd love to know more about your experience.

# MODULE 3

# PREPARING YOUR HOME

*"People who care about animals tend to care about people. They don't care about animals to the exclusion of people. Caring is not a finite resource and, even more than that, it's like a muscle: the more you exercise it, the stronger it gets."*

—Jonathan Safran Foer

# PART I

# ITEMS YOU WILL NEED

CONGRATULATIONS ON ADOPTING YOUR NEW DOG! The real fun begins now as you introduce your newest family member to your home. In this module, you learn about some basic items you should have before your dog arrives, as well as a few things you should do while he's settling into your home. It's fun preparing for your new pup!

As always, however, safety is the main concern. Remember to store away toxic substances and foods in cabinets with a proper locking system. Products that we wouldn't normally think of as appealing, like anti-freeze, can be very appealing to dogs and potentially life threatening. It might seem silly, but it's a good idea to get down on your hands and knees to identify possible hazards from their vantage point. Adopt-a-pet.com offers pet-proofing tips[Δ] that will help keep your pet safe and your belongings intact.

Here's a quick checklist of some common items you will need before or soon after your dog arrives. If you live near water or woods, consider the extra precautions you will have to take to keep him safe, like fencing around a pool, life jackets if you go boating, and other preparations for walks in heavily wooded areas.

- Collar
- Harness or Head Collar
- Non-retractable Leash
- Tags and Microchipping
- Dog License
- Food and Water Bowls
- High-quality Food
- Treats
- Toys
- Poop bags
- Dog Bed
- Crate

Optional:

- Dog-friendly Yard
- Leash Tie-outs
- Baby Gate
- Furniture Protection
- Pet Spray
- Lint Roller

- Microfiber Mop/Vacuum
- Puppy Housebreaking Pads
- Dog Brush and Shampoo
- Placemat for Dog Bowls
- Doggie Door

## Items Explained:

- **Collar**: Every dog needs a durable collar that doesn't fray. Some people take their dog's collar off when at home so it doesn't catch on anything. I worry that my dogs might escape while their collars are off (and thus be without ID) and sometimes I use the collars to pull our dogs away from each other in a scuffle, so we leave them on at all times. Be sure to wait until you adopt your dog before purchasing a collar to make sure it fits properly.

- **Harness or Head Collar**: Your dog may need a special harness or no-pull head collar for walking if he is a strong breed that pulls or if he has a small head and could slip out of a regular collar. We use a head collar for both of our dogs as an alternative to a harness or prong collar.
  * I prefer the Walk 'n Train brand head collar because it not only fits around the dog's head, but also offers an additional latch onto his collar which our trainer, Lynn Medlin of Dog Town Dog Training△ recommends. If the part around the snout comes off, you still have control of your dog. When used properly, it works like a horse lead reducing the dog's body weight by a third. So walking a 60-pound dog is now more like walking a 20-pound dog and much easier to handle.

  \* It is common for dogs to take as long as a couple of weeks to get used to head collars. Take care not to jerk on the leash, which could harm his neck in any collar. Please refer to an article by Jeff Stallings of Better Nature Dog Training (betternaturedogtraining.com) who wrote an article[Δ] all about head collars with more options and in-depth explanation.

  \* To get our dog Ninja used to it, we followed the video instructions and started by putting the loop around his face for a few seconds while giving him a treat. We gradually increased the time to 30 seconds, then a minute and so on. He eventually wore it around the house for a few minutes on leash while we distracted him with treats to reinforce that wearing the collar is positive. We were then able to take him on walks wearing it.

  \* People unfamiliar with this type of head collar often mistake it for a muzzle since it is worn around the snout, but it does not offer any bite protection at all. Dogs are able to eat and drink while wearing it.

  \* Note about prong collars: Some dogs are trained and comfortable in a prong collar, and there are trainers that still believe they are a fine solution for strong dogs. Lynn Medlin helped us transition Ninja from the prong collar that he was wearing when we adopted him to the head collar that he uses now. She is very un-

> Note about muzzles: Some dogs may be leash reactive or have a strong fear of strangers, requiring a muzzle. Please consult a professional trainer on the proper usage of a muzzle.

derstanding though, of families who insist on using what works for them and shared, "While it's not my first choice, if a prong collar is the only solution a family can come up with, I'd rather know that the dog is at least being walked."

- **Leash**: Plan to purchase a six-foot, sturdy, non-retractable leash. The leash should have a loop that you can wrap around your wrist and then hold the length of the leash in your hand. I just purchased a new one that is adjustable, so I can make it even shorter than six feet. You have much more control over your dog when you can pull him close to you quickly.
  * Retractable leashes pose many potential dangers, including getting tangled or loss of control if another dog comes up suddenly or if your dog runs into the street. When your dog is within 6 feet of you, you have much greater control while walking him. I invite you to learn more about the hazards of retractable leashes. Please read the article by Dr. Karen Becker at Healthy Pets/Mercola.com called "Why I don't Recommend Retractable Leashes."△
  * If you plan to walk your dog after dark, a reflective leash or a lighting system (like blinking lights on your dog's collar) will make you more visible.

- **Tags**: In case your dog is lost or stolen, they will need to have identification tags. Your dog will have a few tags: A legible ID tag, a city license tag (if required) and a proof of rabies vaccine tag. If you plan to move, update your information with the microchip company as well as in a database like PetHub's.△ Do this prior to your move in case he escapes before he is accustomed to his new home. There are different quality tags—some that fade quickly and others that are guaranteed to last the life of your dog. Boomerang Tags[Δ] was recently recommended to me.

*"At a time when one in three pets will go missing at some point in their lives, PetHub's revolutionary digital ID tags provide a more advanced tool to get pets home safely and quickly. In fact, 97% of PetHub recovered pets are home the same day, most in just a few short hours."*

—Lorien Clemens,
Director of Marketing and Business Development, PetHub
www.pethub.com

- **Microchip**: It is also highly recommended that you have your dog microchipped. A microchip is a teeny tiny chip inserted under his skin that can be scanned at a vet or a shelter to identify your dog. This is a requirement for most rescue organizations and shelters and increasingly so for many cities.

Please visit PetHub.com for a helpful infographic from Pet Hub and Barkandswagger.com on Dog Theft Prevention.[Δ]

- **Dog License**: Your city may require that your dog be licensed. Usually that means you go to the city office (often at your local shelter) with proof of vaccinations and pay a fee. In some cities it is mandatory that your dog be spayed or neutered. In others, you get a fee reduction if they are. The license must be renewed annually. Always check local laws to make sure you are in compliance. I applied at the Animal Control office in my town and renew by mail annually.

- **Dog Bowls:** Dogs need one bowl for food and another for fresh water. For large or long-eared breeds, consider raised bowls. Metal or ceramic is recommended over plastic for everyday use. [Note: For dogs susceptible to bloat, a raised bowl is not recommended. More about bloat in the feeding section later in this module.]

  * Your dog should have fresh water at all times. My son changes the water bowl twice daily, and I remind him to rinse it out every time.

- **High-quality Food:** You will need to continue feeding your new dog whatever he was fed at the shelter, foster home or other boarding facility. If you change his food to a higher quality, home cooked or raw food, plan to do so gradually over a period of days or even weeks to avoid stomach upset. Ask your veterinarian for specific food-weaning guidelines.

  * Feeding guidelines are a popular question from new dog parents. How much food and how often? Soft or hard? What is the healthiest option and where can I find it?

*"Calculate your monthly budget, and figure out exactly how much you can and are willing to spend on dog food each month. Then, buy the best food you can for that budget."*

—Maggie Marton, Oh My Dog blog[Δ]

For more about feeding, please visit ohmydogblog.com

  * Our very first trainer recommended feeding twice daily a mix of kibble and canned food to emulate the food your dog would find in the wild—a combination of meat and crunch. She also recommended mixing a little water in

with the kibble to make a more digestible gravy, so that's what we do to this day. We also add in a little pumpkin or sweet potato because that is good for their bellies.

* Many experts suggest feeding adult dogs twice daily (and puppies three to four times daily while older dogs may choose to eat less frequently). Feeding twice daily helps prevent your dog from gobbling down food, which could cause bloat. Large dogs are particularly prone to bloat when they eat too quickly which can result in death. You can read more about bloat from veterinarians in an article that originally appeared at petMD.com.<sup>Δ</sup>

* Veterinarians recommend that you feel your dog's ribs to help you gauge their optimal weight. To help you evaluate your dog, you can consult a handy guide from Animal Emergency and Critical Care Center of Brevard.<sup>Δ</sup> Excessive weight places strain on his joints, and can affect his heart and overall health, which can be especially problematic as he ages. Likewise, if your dog is too skinny or malnourished, ask your vet how to safely get him to his optimal weight.

* It is not advised that you leave a food bowl out all day long for your dog to graze, because they tend to overeat. Feeding your dog in a controlled manner also establishes boundaries and allows you to use food as a training tool. If you notice a change in your dog's eating habits, you should always investigate with your vet.

*"When we feed our dogs, that seemingly mundane act is one of our most powerful training tools. Making the dogs wait for a release command like 'OK' is an exercise of leadership that strengthens the animals' security in knowing someone is in control of their world.*

*Free feeding a dog strips us of a very powerful tool to gently and consistently remind our pets that we are in control and they can look to us for guidance in all situations."*
—Kelley Kemp, Trainer and Owner, Bakersfield Dog Behavior
www.bakersfielddogbehavior.com

Some families choose to cook for their dog or offer a raw or vegan diet. All diets require diligence to ensure that your dog is still getting all the necessary nutrients.

*"One question new pet parents ask me is 'what should we feed our puppy?' We chose to transition our puppies to a species appropriate, raw food diet, which incorporates the right balance of raw muscle meat, organ meat, and bones. Raw feeders have reported fewer health issues, better temperament, and longer lives with their dogs. To learn more, speak with a holistic veterinarian experienced in the raw food diet on how to best transition your new best friend."*
—Kimberly Gauthier,
Dog Nutrition Blogger, Keep The Tail Wagging
www.keepthetailwagging.com

The American Holistic Veterinary Medical Association (AH-VMA)[Δ] has a listing of holistic veterinarians you can search to find one closest to you if you are interested in learning more about a raw food diet.

    *   Some of the best-known brand dog foods contain grains (which dogs don't need in their diet), are processed overseas or have had a recall. For some guidance, you can consult a list of dog foods from Reviews.com[Δ] that were analyzed based on a myriad of variables.

* When our dog T-bone was sick he stopped eating store bought food, so I cooked for him for months. When he was feeling better, and I realized that I was cooking more for my dogs than for my family, my dogs went back to high quality store bought food.
* I keep my dog food consistent, though lately many experts have been encouraging variety.
* WebMD.com^Δ offers a more in-depth article on dog feeding.
* Be sure to ask your vet for specific feeding instructions for your dog.

*"We treat our pets as a member of our family. Feeding them natural foods and treats (ideally made in the US or other quality sources) ensures your pets' health, wellness and longevity. Make sure you have a clear understanding of how to read ingredient labels and stay away from unnecessary food-dyes, chemicals, fillers and preservatives."*

—Lisa Iszard, Owner,
Tumbleweed & Eddie's Natural Pet Treat Company
www.tumbleweedandeddies.com

• **Treats**: If you just adopted your dog, getting a treat from you may be one of the best things that has ever happened to him. It's a great way to express love. For a food-motivated dog, treats are terrific training rewards. Don't feed him too many treats though, because you don't want an overweight dog (see the High Quality Food section for guidelines). Be sure to choose US or Canadian sourced high-quality treats.
* I still use treats as positive reinforcement when I walk my dogs. I break the treats up into very small pieces so they get

the benefit of the training treat, but not too many calories at a time. Some people use their dog's kibble for training. For more finicky dogs, tiny pieces of high value treats like cheese or hot dogs can be effective for training.

*"We believe that all dogs should have access to safe and nutritious food regardless of their situation. After we lost one of our four-legged family members to a pet food recall, we made it our mission to provide only safe and trusted food that we prepared for the remaining members of our fur family. We also began sharing our story and our passion with other pet parents and One Dog Organic Bakery was born."*

—Veronica Glynn, Owner, One Dog Organic Bakery

- **Toys**: Toys are a good idea, especially if you have a dog that likes to chew or who has never had a toy before. They will feel like they hit the jackpot!

*"One thing that helped was a toy. Joey didn't seem to understand how to play. I had gotten him a stuffed dog with an elastic band inside so it stretched when tugged. After some efforts on my part, he fell in love with that toy. It became something we could do together that he enjoyed."*

—Jeannette Hartman, Fido Universe
www.fidouniverse.com

* If you already have another dog, be sure to supervise them while playing to make sure they don't get into a squabble over a toy. Our dogs only get toys when we're home and the toys go into a basket when we go out.

* Be aware that playing tug-of-war with your dog can be dangerous if he tries to grab the rope too close to your hand. Years ago it was suggested that we use a long rope toy to play tug-of-war which makes sense because it puts more space between your hand and the dog's mouth.

* Children should not be allowed to play tug-of-war with dogs, as they could accidentally get bitten and should always be supervised around dogs, especially new dogs in the home. (Please see more about kids and dogs below in the Safety Section.)

* Be sure not to give your dog any type of bone that he can choke on, or any toy he can destroy immediately. Dogs with strong jaws can tear open a supposedly durable toy in just minutes and potentially choke on a squeaker or other foreign object. Always supervise your dog so that he doesn't ingest anything he shouldn't. While still popular, rawhide bones can be very dangerous. Some contain poisons and often cause gastrointestinal problems including blockages. There are many alternatives like antler chews or Bully sticks.

*"Baked bones splinter and rawhide is full of chemicals. When dogs gnaw on antler chews, the chews do not splinter like bones. The chewing action grinds the antler into a powder that is chock-full of natural calcium, phosphorous and additional minerals. Antler chews are a good choice for the big chewer in your home and have the added advantage of assisting in keeping your pooch's teeth clean as well."*
—Cindy Dunston Quirk, Founder, Scout & Zoe's Antler Chews
www.scoutandzoes.com

* Again, be careful when offering any chew treats to your dog.
* I also recommend toys that you can stuff treats into that allow your dog to "play a game" to retrieve it. An example is stuffing peanut butter (a high value treat) in a hollow Kong®Δ toy, or dog puzzles, which also offer mental exercise.
* Remember not to use your personal belongings, even an old sweatshirt or socks, as a toy because your dog can't discern which is his toy and which is your favorite cozy sweatshirt not to be messed with. Plus, shredded clothing can get lodged in his stomach, which could possibly lead to a blockage requiring surgery.

• **Poop Bags**: Always be a responsible neighbor and carry pet cleanup bags where required. There are three biodegradable brands that I recommend and use: BioBag®,Δ Outward Hound's® Pooch Pickups®,Δ and Earth Rated®,Δ offering benefits like a lavender smell to help mask odors, easy tie handles and/or a dispenser that you can hook onto your leash.

• **Bed**: Every dog deserves a cozy dog bed to sleep on.
* Our dogs sleep for part of the night on our bed, part of the night in my kid's rooms and part of the night on a dog bed next to our bed. It's like musical beds.
* Many families don't wish to share their bed with their dog, so a dog bed is fine. It is a personal preference, though don't be surprised if you are a person who swears that their dog will never be allowed to sleep in your bed and they wind up under the covers with you!
* We have two types of dog beds at home. The thinner, lighter one fits perfectly in the crate. (See crate information be-

53

low.) Our dog Ninja likes to steal these portable beds out of the crate and leave them all around the house. We also have larger, sturdier beds that stay in one place that are more difficult for a dog to destroy.

   *  Dogs like beds that have a back or ridge that offer an enclosed feeling, which mimics a den atmosphere.

   *  Some families plan to have their new dog sleep in a bathroom or in a laundry room and many dogs are just fine that way. Other dogs resist and make a lot of noise when left alone. Many trainers and rescue groups recommend crating your dog at bedtime until he settles in. This way he can't roam around the house or make a mess while you are sleeping. You may decide that you like having him nearby in a crate, or you may decide later on that he can sleep on your bed. Starting him in the crate offers you options and peace of mind from the beginning.

- **Crate**: What is a crate? A crate is a large pet-safe enclosure, also called a pet carrier or kennel. There are three common styles of crates: fabric, wire bars or molded plastic.
  -  *  Some dogs are already crate-trained as it is a natural environment for most dogs. Dogs like the cozy, confined space and often choose to go into their crate even when it's not required.

*"Dogs often find crates instinctually comforting. The covered crate mimics a den in the wild in the way that wild dogs, coyotes and wolves live. It provides security, peacefulness and a quieter, darker place alone where they can go when they are tired, feeling ill, don't want to be bothered by kids or stressful situations like parties, fireworks or workmen in the house."*

—Leela Ruiz, Owner, Dog and House
www.dogandhouse.com

*   There is some controversy about the use of crates. The concern is that people leave their dogs in the crate for hours on end. The dogs aren't socialized or exercised and then it's not a positive training tool, it's abuse and neglect. Moreover, a crate should always represent a safe and positive environment, not a punishment tool. Like any aspect of pet parenting, there needs to be some common sense and humanity exercised. Why would you get a dog and then just stick him in a crate for hours and hours? I'm confident that if you've gotten to this point in the book, you are committed to loving your new dog as a part of your family.

Adopt-a-Pet.com[Δ] offers advice in a blog on how to crate train your puppy or dog.

*   If you're not sure if your dog is crate-trained and you'd like for him to be, borrow a crate from a friend and try it out. You can follow the proper guidelines and make the crate into a safe haven for your pup.
*   Crates are great for times when you are going out and don't want to leave your new pup with access to your whole house. It's also effective when you want to keep him from jumping or running out the door when someone comes over. When the doorbell rings, our dogs go right in their crates, and then we have a whole routine for meeting guests.
*   The crate can also be used as a place of recovery if your dog has a health challenge, an injury, or right after any kind of surgery.
*   Be sure not to leave your dog in a crate for more than a few hours at a time (some experts say 2-3 hours, others say 4 is OK), except when sleeping overnight. Some dogs will

eventually go right into their crate at night and you won't even have to close the door.

\* Many crates come with hard metal rungs and bars and while many dogs enjoy the crate, always make sure there is comfortable bedding inside.

\* We've had a few Houdini dogs who escaped from crates that we thought were properly shut. Something to be on the lookout for.

\* Be sure to choose the proper sized crate for your dog so that he can stand up, turn around and lay down comfortably in it. Some crates have a feature that allows you to expand it as your dog grows—a feature to consider if you are adopting a dog who is not yet full grown (especially a large breed dog).

Please consult a professional in positive crate training for your dogs.

## Optional Items:

• **Dog-friendly Yard**: If you do have a yard, or other dog-friendly outdoor space be sure your fences are well maintained. Periodically check for holes in the fence and for any digging underneath. If your new dog can jump, the fence should be high enough to contain him around the entire perimeter of your yard. Check fence heights, but also get down on your hands and knees and make sure there are no other dog level hazards or holes. Keep a close eye on your pup while he is settling into his new environment. Remember that your dog is a new family member and the safe yard is for recreation, or even extended time during moderate weather, but not where he should live day in and day out.

*"We don't always know the past of animals in rescue. Often times they are very fearful of their new environment and are a flight risk until they become familiar with their new home. This might take a few weeks or longer. Patience and vigilance is key...[and] ALWAYS make sure your dog has proper identification. While microchipping is great to assist in recovering lost pets for owners, a visible tag is the fastest way to reunite a lost dog with his/her owner."*

From *The Animal Rescuer's Perspective on Pet Safety*[Δ]
—Carole Feeny and Kristin Waters, Project Blue Collar
www.projectbluecollar.com

A dog-friendly yard keeps your dog inside and also doesn't have anything poisonous he can consume, or touch, or bodies of water he can accidentally fall into. Remind any gardeners, employees or other people who routinely enter your property to properly latch gates and doors behind them. For more ideas on creating a dog-friendly yard, check out an article from Adopt-a-Pet.com.[Δ]

> Many dogs, even some large breeds, live happily in apartment buildings. Whatever your arrangement, just be sure your home is dog-proofed and your dog has access to fresh air and exercise regularly.

Cornell University's College of Agriculture and Life Sciences[Δ] offers a comprehensive list of poisonous plants, indoor and out.

- **Leash Tie-outs**: In addition to a crate, you can have leash tie-outs throughout the house. A leash tie-out is simply a leash attached to a table leg, or other sturdy furniture, that you can hook onto your dog's collar in a pinch to keep him in one place. Again, please use common sense. This doesn't mean you leave a dog tied to a table all day, or tied up where he cannot be monitored. But, when used properly, it is a great training tool that allows your dog to be in the same room with the family yet keeps him from getting into trouble or wreaking havoc.

- **Baby Gate**: You can also use a baby gate for when you cannot offer your full attention or to confine a dog to a specific room or area. This is particularly effective because a new dog can still be a part of the scene without getting into trouble in the off-limits area.

- **Furniture Protection**: Every family has different rules about which furniture is off-limits. To keep your furniture clean and intact you can cover it with old blankets or towels until your dog learns to stay off. Wire hangers on a sofa can be a deterrent and sprays like bitter apple can deter chewing on table and chair legs. Sometimes the chewing is natural puppy teething, other times it's adult dogs experiencing separation anxiety. (See Module 5 for more about separation anxiety.) Ultimately, you want your dog to be comfortable with or without you around. This comes with time, patience, training and vigilance in protecting your belongings.

- **Non-Toxic Pet Spray and Cleaning Products**: Even if a dog is potty trained, accidents still happen. Sometimes they happen because the dog is stressed in a new environment. Other times, despite your best efforts, your dog will find some yummy food that they are not supposed to have and potentially get sick.

    Our dog Ninja counter surfs, so when we go out we have to close everything up. Recently, I was preparing for a big holiday dinner and left some vegetable bouillon on the counter. It was tucked all the way in the back but he managed to get it down anyway. (Seriously, vegetable bouillon?) There is a ton of sodium in the bouillon and he must have drunk a ton of water to quench his thirst and ended up going potty in the house. I was lucky it wasn't anything worse and that he didn't seem to have any other side effects.

He managed of course to pee all over the living room rug (even though the majority of the house is hardwood) requiring lots of towels and carpet spray. We use Naturally It's Clean™△ brand, which is a non-toxic cleaner made with natural ingredients found in the local health store. There are a few different brands that will work just fine. Be sure to use non-toxic cleaning solutions all throughout your home not only for your dog's health but for yours as well!

More about counter surfing in Module 5.

- **Lint Roller**: Some dogs shed. And some dogs shed a lot. I have a black dog and a tan dog so you can always find some dog hair on me no matter what I'm wearing. We have lint rollers in the house, though regular tape will do in a pinch.

*"Pet hair is something that I've come to consider like jewelry—rarely do I go out in public without some on."*
—Shawna Schuh, President,
Women in the Pet Industry Network
www.womeninthepetindustry.com

- **Microfiber Mop/Vacuum**: I used to use a disposable microfiber sheet and mop system to sweep up dog hair on our hardwood floors. I switched to a fabric mob cover that gets washed which is more eco-friendly. Most people already have a broom or a regular vacuum, but shedding dogs often require the convenience of a special dry mop that attracts fur, or even something fancy like a Roomba®△ which I just received as a Mother's Day gift.

- **Puppy House-Breaking Pads**: These are great for young puppies who aren't yet housetrained. They are absorbent pads and you can teach your dog to potty on them. Please see Module 4 for information about housetraining your new dog.

- **Dog Brush and Dog Shampoo**: Dog shampoo is specially formulated for their coats. Do not use human shampoo on your dog. (Please see below for more information about bathing and grooming.) It's a good idea to have a brush even if you don't plan on bathing your dog at home so you can brush him regularly. There are different kinds of brushes for different types of fur.

- **Placemat for Under Bowls**: I use fairly heavy-duty placemats (sold in pet supply stores) under my dogs' food and water bowls. When they were younger they were messier eaters. Ninja is still a messy drinker so the placemat catches at least some of the mess.

- **Doggie Door**: For some families, having a doggie door can be helpful. Before installing a dog door that could be used when you aren't supervising, be sure your yard is secured from predatory animals as well as people who could potentially harm your dog. While not a replacement for companionship or exercise, a doggie door could work well in your home.

*"A dog door is one way to make your home more pet-friendly. While you are gone all day at work, he can go outside to play, go potty, watch the birds, etc. In 10 years of installing pet doors no one has ever called me to take it out. And when my clients move, they request a dog door in their new home too."*
—Erin Provancha, Owner, Tucson Dog Doors
www.tucsondogdoors.com

Tuscon Dog Doors△ offers a list of dog door benefits in case you are considering one for your home.

# WHAT YOU WILL NEED TO DO

- Vet visit
- Locate emergency vet (just in case)
- Emergency kit
- Bath or Grooming
- Name
- Sign up for training

- **Vet Visit**: Before your dog comes home (or immediately after), make an appointment with a trusted veterinarian for a complete checkup. Be sure to ask questions in the same way you would if it were your own health. If you aren't sure about a treatment or suggestion they are making, get clarification or a second opinion. This is the time to give your vet your dog's vaccination records as well as microchip information for them to store in their database. When your dog goes in for his annual check ups, the vet can scan his chip to make sure it is still working. Here's a little about some of the common topics you may discuss with your vet at the first visit.

**Basic Vaccinations**:
- ☐ Rabies (given every 3 years)
- ☐ Bordatella

☐ Parvo

☐ Distemper

\* Your vet will know the schedule for each vaccine. You can inquire about any location-specific vaccines for your area of the country as well.

\* A lesser-known and slightly more expensive alternative to vaccinations is titering, though this is only available for certain vaccinations. Some people prefer to titer, which avoids the risk of potential negative vaccine reactions.

*"Titering means submitting a blood sample [drawn by your vet] to determine whether your dog has enough antibodies to ensure his immunity against particular diseases... The experts seem to be of one mind on this: Titers are useful in legal and regulatory settings (for travel, for example) to determine whether an animal has ever received a vaccine for a disease like rabies. Titers do NOT, however, denote protection against a given disease."*
Excerpted from an article that originally appeared at petMD. com. For the complete article to help you decide whether titering is right for you and your dog, please visit that article at petMD.com.△

\* My dog T-bone had an allergic reaction to the rabies vaccination. Fortunately the veterinary professionals were monitoring him and were able to stabilize him. Since rabies is a required vaccination where I live, our vet found a different strain and method of administration the next time it was due and he was fine.

Your vet can also help you with flea and tick control and heartworm prevention.

**Fleas**: Fleas can trigger other diseases and should be taken more seriously than just a nuisance.

* We used to use Advantage® brand topical flea control. Then it seemed to stop working for us. We then tried an oral flea medication but my dogs got sick from it. I read online that some dogs had died using that particular medication. Now we spray them down with a natural flea repellent before they go for walks, use a non-toxic flea spray or powder in their bedding and bathe them more frequently during flea season. I am now also trying a veterinarian recommended (not so natural) product called Vectra 3D®. I prefer natural products when possible, but sometimes it is necessary to get the fleas under control with a prescribed medication before you have a full infestation. It is no fun trying to get fleas out of your carpet (or bed!) at home. Your veterinarian can recommend the appropriate flea control products for your dog.

* An article that originally appeared on petMD.com offers some fabulous natural flea remedies.^Δ Your favorite pet store may also recommend a natural product for you to try.

**Ticks**: Check your dog for ticks, especially if you live in a wooded area, as ticks can cause serious diseases such as Rocky Mountain spotted fever, or Lyme disease. If you live in a high tick zone, you may wish to add a tick preventative. Learn the "10 Ways to Remove a Tick From a Dog"^Δ including tips on prevention in an article that originally appeared on petMD. com

**Heartworm**: Heartworm is different than the worms you see from fleas. Heartworm is transmitted through mosquitoes and is a potentially deadly disease. There is a monthly preventative medicine you can administer called Heartgard®. It is sold in a cookie form and my dogs love it.

**Worms**: If you notice worms in your dog's stool when he comes home from the shelter, there's a good chance he's been eating his fleas. But there are a whole host of other worms your dog could have including roundworm as well as other parasites, so your vet will likely do a complete work up. If you discover anything unusual, including diarrhea or vomiting between scheduled visits, let your vet know. Sometimes it's as simple as bringing in a stool sample to the veterinary office.

**Skin Issues**: There are many reasons why your dog may have skin issues ranging from environmental causes, poor nutrition, diseases and behavioral issues. A common skin ailment for dogs who were previously on the streets is demodex mange which is a contagious disease caused by mites causing itching, hair loss and scabs. Petfinder.com△shares an article with more information about skin problems.

*"When we adopted our Dalmatian Rosie we realized she had all sorts of skin issues that became infected, including staph infections. We tried remedy after remedy and tons of antibiotics and she would seem better for a bit, but after years of tests and trials, we tried Zyrtec® and that seems to work the best. She's highly allergic to just*

*about everything including human hair! Apparently it's common for white dogs with short coats to have these types of skin issues."*
—Kelly Syers and Josh Raphaelson,
Dog Parents to Rescued Rosie and Rocky

* If your new dog is licking himself excessively, it may also be stress due to the new environment in your home. Speak with your vet and/or a trainer or behaviorist for suggestions.
* Every spring my dogs get super itchy and start licking "hot spots" requiring topical medicated spray as well as oral anti-itch medication. Additionally, both of my dogs were itchy a few years ago (not in spring) and I learned then that in addition to seasonal allergies, chicken could be an irritant. When we switched to beef, they stopped scratching! Always check with your vet who can look for the underlying cause.

**Supplements, Medications and More:**
* Many supplements and medications come in some type of tasty cookie form. Others are in regular pill or liquid form.
* My dogs take a bunch of pills for orthopedic issues that we shove into their wet food. Sometimes we forget and then I stick the pill in a wad of peanut butter, which they love. Cheese is often used as a high-value treat for pilling and there are also specially created treats used to administer pills, such as Greenies™ Pill Pockets®.△
* If your dog requires any eye or ear drops, or any shots (like subcutaneous fluids) have the vet tech show you how to administer it properly and make sure you are comfortable doing this before you leave the clinic.

* Another "fun" experience is taking a dog's temperature. My dog T-bone needed his temperature monitored daily which, as you may know, is done rectally. T-bone was a champ and it didn't bother him at all. Ninja, our newest dog, however, recently needed his temperature taken at the vet and suffice it to say it was a challenge. Be sure if you plan to do this at home that the vet tech shows you how, and you use the proper type of thermometer. Normal temperature for a dog is 101-102.5 degrees Fahrenheit.

**Spay and Neuter:**
* Most dogs are spayed or neutered before being released from the shelter or rescue group, unless they are too young. If your new pup is too young, you may be allowed to take him home and then bring him back for surgery. Some female puppies can get pregnant as young as five months. So make sure your female dog is spayed as soon as possible and don't let her come in contact with unneutered males in case she's in heat.
* There is some controversy surrounding spay and neuter procedures. Opponents believe that the dogs' health may be compromised in other ways. While there is merit to this conversation, there are so many health benefits of spaying and neutering and the obvious benefit of reducing the number of unwanted dogs. Low cost and free spay and neuter are available in most communities. You can check the ASPCA® database[Δ] for super "Low Cost Spay-Neuter Programs."
* If your dog recently had surgery, or has any other wound or irritation, he may be required to wear an Elizabethan collar (or E-collar) to make sure he doesn't lick or pull at his stitches or wound. These are the plastic looking cones that

you sometimes see dogs wearing. There are many flexible types of collars these days, though wearing anything that limits his visibility or movement may be uncomfortable for him. If your dog refuses to wear it and you've tried them all, ask your vet about different options.

**Coat**: A shiny coat comes from a healthy diet and good grooming. When you first adopt your dog, he may be dirty or matted and a bath might be all he needs to get shiny. But there could be underlying issues as well. If you are feeding your dog a high quality diet, and bathing and brushing him regularly yet there are still fur or skin issues, see your veterinarian.

**Teeth**: Your vet may recommend a professional cleaning if your dog's teeth have been neglected. Traditionally your dog will be anesthetized (which I prefer to avoid) but there are vets and other veterinary professionals who can do a thorough cleaning while your dog is awake. Be sure to ask about that option.

Again, these are just some of the common health topics to consider at first. With annual check ups and visits when something seems amiss you should be able to get answers to your questions.

- **Emergency Vet**: Know where the nearest emergency after-hours vet is located, just in case. Post their address and phone number in your home and make sure the dog sitter has it when you are out.
  - \* Here are five phone numbers every dog family should have handy, according to the Dogington Post. The full printable article can be found at the Dogingtonpost.com.<sup>Δ</sup>

**National Animal Poison Control Center: 1 888 426 4435**
**Spay/Neuter Helpline: 1 800 248 SPAY**
**Animal Legal Hotline: (707) 795-2533**
**Emergency Disaster Information Line: 1 800 227 4645**
**Pet Travel Hotline: 1800 545 USDA.**

- **Emergency Kit**: Whether you live in a region prone to tornados, hurricanes or earthquakes (or not) having an emergency kit that includes food and water specifically for your dog is a good idea. See Module 5 for more info about pet first aid. Please visit my website for a handy quick reference Disaster Preparedness Sheet from Pet First Aid and CPR instructor, Denise Fleck, Sunny-dog ink.[Δ]

- **Bath or Grooming**: Once you get home, you may realize that while *you* see your new dog's inner and outer beauty, he could really use a bath! Your vet may even be able to bathe him while he's there for his check up. Ask when you make your first appointment. Your dog will especially need a bath if he has just been brought home from a shelter or if he has fleas. Ask for a flea dip treatment if he is being professionally bathed. You can also bathe your dog at home or take your dog to a groomer, doggy dunk, or have a mobile dog-washing service come to you if available.
  * Bathing at home will be most cost-efficient, as it only requires dog shampoo, a brush and some old towels. (Old towels are also good to have around during the rainy season when your dog comes in soaking wet.) Be sure to use shampoo especially formulated for dogs. If your dog is small you can wash him in the sink. Ours have always been at least mid-sized so bathing in a sink is not an option.

* The nice thing about bathing and brushing your dog is that it gives you an opportunity to feel and look for any skin abnormalities that should get checked out by a veterinarian. Make sure you are rubbing him and checking his whole body regularly to make sure everything appears normal between his annual vet check ups. If anything looks suspicious, be sure to show your vet.

* The only time we bathe our dogs ourselves is in the summertime when we can bathe them outside (because bathing in the tub is messy work). Dogs naturally shake their whole body when they are wet to dry themselves off and even outside it can be messy business.

* A doggy dunk is great if you prefer to do it yourself. Most have raised tubs so you don't have to bend over, and detachable water sources, making it easier than bathing in your tub. They also have a short leash that attaches to the tub so your dog doesn't escape mid-bath. It is a relatively inexpensive alternative and they supply aprons, towels and clean up the mess afterwards.

* We have used a mobile groomer in the past. They park a specially outfitted van in front of your home and the dog gets one-on-one treatment. The biggest bonus of mobile grooming is that your dog does not need to stay in a crate while he is waiting for his turn. Mobile

> Denise Fleck of Sunny-dog Ink recommends a weekly full body check. It's a good time to check that your dogs' tags are secured to their collar as well.

groomers are generally more expensive than other grooming options.

\* Nowadays, we take our dogs to a professional groomer who not only bathes and brushes our dogs, but also clips toe nails, does a quick teeth cleaning and expresses (empties) their anal glands. (I know it sounds gross,

> If you notice your dog shaking his head when he is NOT wet, he could be having a problem with his ears and should visit the vet. Our dog T-bone had ear infections requiring ear cleaning and medication, which we were able to do once the vet showed us how. The shake after ear medication (especially when you use a cleaning solution) can get all over you and your furniture, so plan to do that outside if possible.

but for many dogs it needs to be done by an experienced professional on a regular basis. When a dog scootches on the floor, or licks constantly around his butt, that could mean he needs his anal glands expressed.) Always check with your vet.

*"Over 60% of dog owners allow dogs in their beds. Unfortunately, few of them clean their dogs on a regular basis to keep them smell-free and reduce the amount of bacteria and yeast brought inside. Your dog's hygiene regime needs to include regular brushing, and a bath as often as needed (for some breeds it's weekly). The regime may include cleaning yeast coming out of dog's eyes with eye pads,*

*brushing their teeth and trimming nails. When dog owners tell me 'My dog does not need a bath or any of that stuff' I ask them not to take a shower, or brush their hair or clean their teeth for months and let me know how it feels.*

*The high quality of today's grooming products allows dog parents to bring dog hygiene to the next level and ensure a clean dog and a smell-free house."*

—Elena Volnova, Co-Founder, Dog Fashion Spa

www.dogfashion.us

Learn more about dog hygiene from Elena on my website.[Δ]

If you are bathing your dog and clipping his nails at home rather than taking him for professional grooming, make sure not to cut them down too far as that can be painful or cause an infection.

* Ninja bites his own nails, which I learned is not uncommon. Gonzo, on the other hand will only let one groomer handle his paws, (and we've tried many!) so that's where we go for grooming and nail trimming (or we take him to the vet for his nails). It is helpful if you gently and frequently handle your dog's paws when he is new to you, especially if he is a puppy, so he gets used to getting his nails trimmed.
* We bathe our dogs at least monthly and sometimes more often during flea season which roughly starts in spring in Southern California and goes until winter. My dog Ninja the Labrador/Pit Bull mix sheds seasonally and the grooming helps (at least temporarily) to reduce some of the excessive shedding. We tend to brush him more during high shedding times too. Check with a trusted groomer to find out how often a bath or grooming is recommended for

your dog. Remember that dogs who have longer hair, and poodles and poodle mixes, need to be groomed properly and frequently so they don't become matted.

*"Stand back. He's going to shake!"*

An article that originally appeared on petMD.com explains why matting is potentially unhealthy for your dog and what you can do to prevent it.[Δ]

* If your dog encounters a skunk, rolls in something gooey, or swims in fishy smelling water, regular dog shampoo won't cut it. Petfinder.com's, "Tips for Tackling Dog Smells"[Δ] article that originally appeared in *The Adopted Dog Bible* offers recipes and ideas to get Rover smelling like a dog again.

• **Name:** Some pets already have a name that fits them perfectly. Sometimes, though, you'll want to change the name they were given by the people working in the shelter. It's fine to change any pet's name, but if a more mature pet is accustomed to his name you may wish to leave it.

\*    Our dog Ninja was two years old when we adopted him. His name was Jay back then because he had a big white "J" on his black chest. But our first dog (and the namesake of my children's book series) was named JJ, which was too similar. So that, and the fact that Jay just didn't fit, prompted us to consider a new name. We realized after a few days that he was very stealthy (seriously, how does a 65 pound dog with jingly tags sneak up on you?) and we chose to rename him Ninja. The most important thing is that you believe your dog's name fits.

*"When we first brought Sweet Pea home, we were so excited to have our first pet as a family. Once we got her comfortable and showed her around a little, we started the discussion about what to call her. She's a black cocker spaniel with white markings, so we tossed around some cute names that accentuated her looks, and each time we thought of a cute name, we'd call it out and see if she liked it. 'Boots!' Nothing. 'Pepper!' Nothing. 'Shadow!' She just didn't care for anything we tried.*

*Then Robin Williams hit the jackpot. No, he wasn't at our house, but we had the movie 'Popeye' on and he was searching for his missing baby, Sweet Pea. 'Sweet Pea! Oh, Sweet Pea!' called out the young Robin Williams. That was it for our sweet little pup, she came dashing over and sat down at attention, waiting for Robin to say it again.*

*I was intrigued. 'Sweet Pea?' She turned to me as though to say, 'Yes, what is it Ma?' Our dog named herself Sweet Pea!"*

—Elyse Horvath, Founder, Natural Paws
www.naturalpaws.net

*What did you name your dog? I'd love to hear how you came up with it.*

- **Training**: I encourage you to sign your new pup up for puppy training classes so he can learn basic commands and get socialized. Plus it's another opportunity for you to bond. Either a group training class or in-home private training is a good idea. Some rescue organizations will send a trainer to work with your pet immediately after adoption. Though group classes help socialize your dog, you might have to wait a bit longer for a new session to start. An in-home trainer may be immediately available to get the training started sooner. (More about training in Module 5.)

If you don't have a good recommendation from friends, please consult the Association of Professional Dog Trainers (APDT) for a qualified trainer near you.[△]

*"A dog's mind is a terrible thing to waste! I knew I wanted him to know some basic commands (like come—which we're still working on). We went to obedience school and kept taking classes. I enjoyed them for what I learned about dogs and about my dog in particular. I felt like the training gave us a basic vocabulary that helped us understand expectations better."*
—Jeannette Hartman, Fido Universe
www.fidouniverse.com

You might need to do more than what is mentioned in this module to prepare for a senior or special needs dog. See Modules 4 and 5 for more information.

Now that you have an idea of some of the basics you will need, come learn more about training, safety as well as more about exercise and socialization in Module 4!

# MODULE 4

# INTEGRATING YOUR DOG INTO YOUR HOME

*"If you think dogs can't count, try putting three dog biscuits in your pocket and then give him only two of them."*

—Phil Pastoret

# PART I

# GETTING ACQUAINTED

IN THIS MODULE, YOU WILL get comfortable with integrating your new dog into your home, family and neighborhood. You will find information about safety, basic training, exercise, and socialization.

## Patience

The most important thing you will need is patience! Your new dog is getting to know your home, family and possibly other pets in the household and it can be stressful for everyone. Often he'll fit right in, but sometimes it will take a little time to adjust. You will fall into a rhythm.

Plan to spend a lot of time with your dog when he first comes home so that he feels comfortable in his new surroundings and begins to trust you. If you must go out, confine him to a room or crate where he can't destroy anything and only leave him for a short while, especially in the beginning. Remember to consult a professional trainer for specifics on proper crate training. (See Module 3 for more information on crate training.)

*"You do not need to be an expert to handle a difficult situation with your companion. You only need to have the patience and motivation to problem solve and figure out a solution. Find out what best motivates your pet, whether it is a toy, food, or affection. Determine if your pet needs to be distracted and what motivates them to refocus his attention on you or something else. Those two things can make a world of difference in achieving success."*

—Jen deHaan, Found Pixel

www.foundpixel.com

Further, it is common for a new dog's true personality to be suppressed at first. Dogs who were recently spayed or neutered may also be quieter than normal for a few days while healing. Don't be surprised if his personality changes a bit over time.

*"When I picked up my dog at the Amanda Foundation*[△] *to bring him home, he was very quiet. He started trembling when I put him in the car. When he came home, he was very subdued. He didn't bark. He didn't do much exploring. He didn't get on the couch. He was very shut down, stoic. I didn't really know what to do, so I kept taking him out for a walk. Which turned out to be*

*the right thing. It took him about four days to even bark once. I was starting to worry if we would ever build a relationship.*

*I had to learn that after having been on the streets, in a city shelter, on the hot sheet and then taken to the Amanda Foundation, he didn't know what to expect next or how long anything would last. Getting into a daily routine helped. Meeting other neighborhood dogs helped. I just had to be patient and remember that trust and all relationships take time to develop."*

—Jeannette Hartman, Fido Universe
www.fidouniverse.com

We did what Jeannette did and walked our dogs a lot when we first adopted them. (We still do.) Frequent walks allow your dog to potty, expend some energy, spend some time with you and get to know your neighborhood. I don't think our dog Gonzo had much, if any, leash walking experience when we first adopted him, so he was a challenge in the beginning. With consistency and training he figured it out quickly and is great to walk with now. If you need a little help getting your dog to walk properly on a leash, you can get some tips from Adopt-A-Pet.com.△

## Multi-Pet Families

Introducing dogs to a home that already has other pets can be tricky. Some pets accept the newcomer easily, others not so much. You must be respectful of your existing pets' space and be sure they feel safe.

## Tips for Introducing Dog to Dog

To help ensure a seamless transition, your existing dog and a new-comer dog should meet on neutral territory. Often with time they will like, or at least tolerate, each other, though sometimes they just don't jive.

Adopt-a-Pet.com offers step-by-step specifics on how to introduce and walk safely with both dogs.[△]

When our newcomer dog, Ninja, was coming to meet our dog Gonzo for the first time, the rescue organization suggested we meet in our neighborhood, away from the house. Gonzo tried to attack Ninja at first, so it's a good thing we knew to keep our distance. After we walked for a few minutes they both calmed down and we could get a little closer. By the time we got back to our house, they were walking beautifully and were ready to run and play together in the backyard. They've been best buds ever since!

*"When we took Tig to the shelter to meet other dogs we were considering for adoption, the only dog she was relaxed around was Mort. As such, he ended up being our chosen dog. However, once we were home Tig mostly ignored Mort apart from the occasional correction. Two weeks later, when Mort and I were lounging on the couch, Tig showed up out of nowhere and launched into a play bow right in Mort's face. Mort and I were shocked, and despite being an extremely playful dog he didn't know what to do. Tig play bowed again and gently nipped his ear—'I'm ready to play!' And, both of them launched into a frenzied game of chase. From then on they have been the best of friends."*

—Jen deHaan, Found Pixel

www.foundpixel.com

## Tips for Introducing Dog to Cat

While some dogs have a strong prey drive and cannot live with cats, many are fine with and even love them. Adopt-A-pet.com offers a six step process to introduce your dog to a cat.^Δ

Blogger Maggie Marton of Oh My Dog blog had terrific success introducing her new cat, Newt, to her pack of dogs, with a lot of patience, treats and tools like baby gates. The progression of her experience is very relatable and entertaining.

The link to her first post from June 17th, 2013 can be found on my website.^Δ The follow up posts can be found at ohmydogblog.com on July 5th, July 30th and December 11th 2013.

If any pets show aggression be sure to separate them and reintroduce them slowly. Always consult a trainer if you have questions or concerns. Never leave your pets home alone together unless you are sure there is no aggressive behavior present at all.

## Housebreaking

Housebreaking (also known as potty training) will surely test your patience. Puppies and adult dogs who haven't had a stable home environment may require lots of time and effort.

If you are potty training a puppy, set him up for success by taking him outside frequently for walks and potty breaks, especially first thing in the morning, any time he's been in the crate, after eating, playing, or after a training session. Praise him in a very sweet voice when he potties outside. If you have a yard you can also let him out and praise him when he goes in the spot you have designated. It may take up to 20 minutes for your dog to get busy, so plan those extra few minutes into your schedule until he reliably potties outside.

It is important to be consistent with your routine, especially in the beginning. Some people like to start out with housebreaking pads or newspaper to train their puppy to potty inside and then transition them outdoors as they get older and their bladders can hold it longer.

Never punish a dog for having an accident inside. He is just learning what is expected of him and very young puppies physically cannot hold it in. Clean up the mess matter-of-factly and set him up for future success by anticipating his need to eliminate. If you happen to catch your puppy mid-stream, scoop him up and quickly bring him outside to finish his business. This is an opportunity to show him where he is supposed to go and praise him for pottying outside. If you can't be home during the day to walk and let out your dog, consider a dog-walker or doggie daycare. (See Module 5, Part 1 for more information about pet sitters and doggie daycare.)

Gonzo learned how to ring a cowbell that we have hanging by our back door when he wants to go out. It's a cool trick that now impresses our guests. Ninja just walks over to the door, stands by it looking cute, and then we let him out.

For housebreaking your dog or puppy, Adopt-a-Pet.com's blog[Δ] could be very helpful.

*"No and stop it! Get off and sit down! Shut up and stop barking! If that's all you heard, day in, day out, how low would your spirits*

*sink? We know that dogs feel sorrow, they get depressed and the very essence of who they are as a species is threatened by a common predator: Mankind. Here are seven things that are guaranteed to destroy the spirit of your dog:*

- *Scolding him/Yelling at him/Rubbing his nose in waste for relieving himself in the house*
- *Hitting him*
- *Punishing with a 'Kennel' Time Out*
- *Taking his food or treats away while he is eating*
- *Not walking or engaging in quality time*
- *Leaving him alone for inordinate amounts of time*
- *Otherwise allowing him to suffer*

*Though these are not pleasant reminders to read, they are all too true. If a dog you know is being harmed, speak up, do something, and/or tell someone. A dog's life just might depend on it."*

Excerpted from an article by Carol Bryant, founder of FidoseofReality.com and Wigglebutt Warriors® Please find the complete post on my website.<sup>Δ</sup>

Some dogs who are technically house trained may be super stressed while transitioning, so be prepared for some accidents in the beginning.

# MODULE 4 PART II

# KIDS ROLES, EXPECTATIONS AND SAFETY

YOUR KIDS WILL FALL IN LOVE with your new dog and will (hopefully) want to help take care of him. Kids can help with many of the chores involved in pet parenting such as feeding, changing the water bowl daily, brushing your dog's fur and of course spending time playing with and loving your new dog!

Older, more responsible kids (teenagers if your dog is big or feisty) can walk and possibly help administer medicine. At any age, children can join on a family walk, which is a bonding time and exercise for everyone. Helping out with your new dog gives your child a sense of responsibility and accomplishment and also helps out the family. The most important consideration though is safety around dogs. According to the CDC, most dog bites occur in kids ages 5-9, so please do your homework and prepare your home.

*"Children need to be taught empathy, compassion and kindness at an early age with animals, humans and the environment. A child with these traits has greater self-esteem and awareness, which also leads to academic success. While teaching children to love and respect animals, it is important to teach them to read dog body language to maintain the safety of the beautiful interaction.*

*When our students work with dogs at the shelter, the top rules are: 'no hands through the kennels and no putting their faces close to the dogs while training.'"*

—Virginia Schifiano Hamilton, CHES, Teacher, Founder of Canine Commandos and Aim Humane www.caninecommandos.com

## Safety and Bite Prevention for the Whole Family

The most accessible resource I've found for child safety around dogs comes from Leah Hatley and Justine Schuurmans of TheFamilyDog. com. They offer fantastic videos that teach in a fun and approachable way.

*"Unfortunately kids and dogs don't come just 'knowing' the right way to behave around each other. So you can't just 'supervise' and hope for the best—you have to TEACH TEACH TEACH! And to be fair—most parents really want to get it right. The problem is that often all the focus is on the dog instead of training the kids too.*

*The family dog has a much better shot at success when parents take the time to teach their kids the ground rules and how to understand dog body language too. Acting kindly and respectfully will help them stay safe and have fun with ALL dogs—starting with their own. Less tolerant dogs are everywhere and unfortunately they don't come with big red flags.*

*Scarily enough, 77% of bites come from family or friends' dogs. So if kids are practicing the right things at home there's a WAY better chance they'll just naturally do what it takes to stay safe with ANY dog they meet. That's why we created stopthe77.com, a*

*fun, educational website that has everything parents need to teach their kids how to live happily and safely with dogs."*
—Leah Hatley and Justine Schuurmans, APDT and
CPDT-KA certified trainers and Co-Owners,
The Family Dog
www.thefamilydog.com

I highly recommend that you spend some time at The Family Dog. com<sup>Δ</sup> "Dog Training for the Whole Family" and Stop the 77.com<sup>Δ</sup> where you will find the best videos that teach kids the dos and don'ts.

Every dog is capable of biting, but with proper socialization, training (people and dogs!) and exercise, you can minimize the chances. There are many reasons why a dog might bite, such as fear or injury. Doggone Safe.com<sup>Δ</sup> is another resource to aid you in dog bite prevention.

Safety is a top priority for the whole family. Everyone in your house should know proper etiquette and basic handling techniques to help ensure their safety as well as the dog's. Training in a group or private setting is invaluable.

Below are a few basics to tide you over until you've had time to check out Stopthe77.com, or call the trainer.

## At Home

- Avoid leaving any children alone at home with your new dog until both parties are well acquainted and mature enough.
- Teach children to be aware of signs that a dog is stressed. Robin Bennett, Certified Professional Dog Trainer (CPDT-KA) has a great infographic showing dog's body language. She also shares why it isn't enough to simply teach kids basic safety and then plan to supervise them. You can find the infographic and article on her website, www.robinkbennett.com.<sup>Δ</sup>

- Children, especially small children, shouldn't run around dogs, as the dog could be frightened or even mistake them for prey.
- Children should not pull tails, poke or hit any dog.
- Avoid approaching dogs from behind so as not to surprise them.

## Out and About

- When out and about, always ask permission before petting another dog.
- Any unfamiliar dog should always be on a leash.
- Before attempting to pet a new dog, allow them to express an interest in meeting you.
- Many dogs don't like being pet on the head because they can't see your hand, which can be frightening for them. Some dogs prefer being pet under the chin, so asking is always prudent.
- Remind children that even though their dog is friendly at home, a dog they've never met might not be as friendly.
- If the person with that dog says it's not a good idea to pet their dog, please respect their wishes.
- Teach children to stand still like a tree if a dog gets loose and runs toward them.
- Children should never approach a dog who is in a car or tied up. When restrained, the fight or flight instinct kicks in and they could become aggressive.

When we adopted our dog Gonzo he was approximately 6 months old. Given that we have two children, naturally we wanted a sweet tempered dog. He seemed sweet at the shelter, otherwise we never would have adopted him. For the first two months he was a typical sweet puppy, but then he became protective of our house and started snapping, particularly at children. This was obviously frightening for us and through the help of a trainer and a behaviorist we learned techniques to deal with him.

Since Gonzo doesn't like when people walk through the front door, he goes into his crate when the doorbell rings. If the guests are "bigger kids" or adults, they come in and we all "meet" Gonzo together (even if they've "met" him 15 times before). When the visitor has a treat in hand, we allow him out of his crate and then they immediately ask him to "sit." The guest then hands him a treat. By using this method, Gonzo learns that his new friends are in control and they come in peace.

We will also sometimes take Gonzo for a walk with this new friend. Most recently our tactic has been to wait a few minutes for Gonzo to get accustomed to having a new person in our home, (hearing their voice and energy) before letting him out of his crate. He's usually less agitated by then. Then we start the treat protocol.

When small children come over, Gonzo stays in his crate or is tethered to a table with a leash tie-out so that he's with us, but can't hurt anyone. This also depends on how old the kids are and whether they can stay away from a kitchen table. If a small friend is visiting for a while, and Gonzo must be confined to his crate, we make sure to take him out for a nice walk afterwards so he can stretch his legs and get a potty break and some love and attention.

It is natural for dogs to be protective of their home and family. By taking the steps we take, we reassure Gonzo that he has a place in the family pack, but the humans take priority.

Important: This is the technique that works for our dog and family though it might not be best for yours.

Some dogs will jump up when they greet a new person. If the dog is small, it's not a big safety concern, but if they are large like my dog Ninja, it can be frightening to suddenly be eye level with a giant black Lab/Pit Bull mix. (He gets some serious vertical air when he jumps.)

Jumping up is bad manners no matter the dog's size and if they knock over a child it could be dangerous. Adopt-a-Pet.com created a slew of videos designed to "Teach Your Dog to Greet Guests Politely Instead of Jumping Up."^Δ

Always consult a professional trainer if you have specific behavioral needs.

## Expecting a Baby?

If you are either expecting a child now or planning for one in the future, there are a number of steps you can take to prepare. We had our dogs before we had our first child. I remember reading about all the different steps you can take before baby comes home to make the transition smooth. Family Paws™ offers a "Dog and Baby Safety Sheet"^Δ and Doggone Safe shares "Baby Safety Around Dogs"^Δ making them both excellent resources to help you prepare for a successful dog and baby experience.

Here I share what worked for our family.

Before our daughter came home, my husband brought home a cloth that we had used with her at the hospital so they could smell her scent. Our dog sitter gave them big walks before we came home so they were mellow. When we brought her home, I greeted them first since I hadn't seen them in a few days. They were curious of course about the new arrival and we introduced her to our dogs and told them she was "their baby." They sniffed but didn't really pay much attention to her. They just wanted our attention along with lots of treats, which we obliged. They still got plenty of walks (I needed to get rid of that baby weight anyway) and their association with her was positive.

We felt that our dogs were family members. While I had no clue how much attention a new baby was going to require, I vowed that my dogs would still get love and attention from me. They were always included and never banished from a room unless the baby was going to sleep.

A friend of mine was so worried that his dog was going to bite his new baby that he insisted on keeping them separate. He never integrated the two and ultimately the dog was neglected until she did in fact bite the baby. My experience shows that most dogs and children can be fine together when integrated properly, so please consult a professional if you have concerns.

## Walking Safety For Kids

Depending on the size and temperament of the dog and the strength and maturity of the child, children can begin to help with dog walking as they get older. If you have a large "Feisty Fido" it is prudent for an adult to maintain the walking responsibility. Often, the issue is how your dog reacts when another critter approaches. Ultimately you want a mature person to make proper decisions in these situations.

Our dog Ninja is a strong mixed breed who is very cat-reactive, and Gonzo is afraid of kids. Walking them can be a challenge when they see a small animal and try to pull away. Only a strong person can handle them in these situations. I am vigilant on walks in anticipation of distractions. We probably look like a pinball machine crossing back and forth across the street avoiding human and animal land mines.

So many dogs, my own included, will react negatively to other dogs when they are on leash due to the fight or flight instinct. In a dog park or open space, however, the instinct doesn't kick in as easily because they aren't restrained by leashes and can run away if they choose. (More about dog parks below.)

While this may seem like a lot of precautions, I encourage you not to be overwhelmed and to remember how magical caring for your new dog will be!

# SAFETY FOR YOUR DOG

SO FAR WE'VE TALKED A LOT about safety for people. Considering your dog's safety is imperative too. Whether it's making sure your yard is properly fenced, feeding him the highest quality food, or choosing a trusted vet or pet sitter, you must take his welfare seriously.

## Extreme Weather

There are a few times a year—like the dead of winter, or the dog days of summer, that necessitate extra care. Each season brings its joys and challenges requiring vigilance as a pet parent.

In winter and summer, dogs need proper protection from the elements. A doghouse outside is insufficient warmth for most dogs during the coldest months, depending on where you live. Further, doghouses can trap heat in the summer, making the air inside even hotter than the air outside. So if your dog will be outside in the summer, make sure he has plenty of shade and fresh water that will remain cool for as long as he is outside. Common sense always prevails.

While many dogs love romping in the snow, prolonged exposure to freezing conditions can be dangerous for your dog's paws. Salts and chemicals used to thaw ice on the street could be harmful to your dog. Pavement or sand in the summer can burn your dog's paws, so test it with the back of your hand for 3-5 seconds before walking your dog.

There are also many campaigns reminding people not to leave their dogs in the car even for a few minutes either in the heat or cold. Don't use the outside temperature as your gauge because your car can quickly heat up, or cool down to extreme temperatures that are unsafe for most pets. Leave them at home while you are running errands.

If you live in a cold climate, see the tips from the American Veterinary Medical Association (AVMA)®Δ on "Cold Weather Pet Safety." Consider a doggie daycare group for indoor play to make sure your dog is getting proper exercise and stimulation in the cold winter months. Remember, dog clothing isn't just for fashion. Some breeds require a warm coat over their natural fur to help keep them protected.

## Holidays

**Winter Holidays**:

Holly, Mistletoe and Poinsettia are all toxic to dogs, so be sure to keep them out of reach during winter holidays. Cornell University's College of Agriculture and Life Sciences offers a comprehensive list of poisonous plants,Δ indoor and out.

**July 4th Fireworks**:

Dogs are more likely to escape when terrified. Be sure your dog is safely inside your home, and that the information on his tag is up to date and securely on his collar just in case. PetHub offers tips to keep your dog safe during fireworks.Δ

**Halloween**:

Halloween can be really fun for kids and families but potentially dangerous for your dog. Most candy is toxic to dogs, so keep it locked away. Some dogs don't mind getting dressed up, but be sensitive to him if costumes are a source of distress.

Having strangers come to your door over and over can be stressful for your dog. Be sure he is in a safe and comfortable environment, either in a quiet room or in his crate during festivities. The ASPCA® offers a complete list of Halloween safety tips on their website.△

# TRAINING, EXERCISE AND SOCIALIZATION

## Basic Training

TRAINING NOT ONLY TEACHES YOUR dog how to behave the way you expect in your home, but it also helps to socialize your dog and strengthen your bond. The ASPCA recommends training and socializing your puppy as early as eight weeks old (once they are fully vaccinated). If you adopt an adult dog, it's still important to make a commitment to his socialization and training. While I suggest a minimum of basic training, many trainers also offer more advanced training classes. You can consult The Association of Professional Dog Trainers (APDT) for a list of dog trainers$^\Delta$ in your area.

## Classes

All of our dogs attended obedience classes whether they came to our family as a puppy or an adult. Ninja and Gonzo, our current furry family members, both required additional training and attended a "Feisty Fido" class (yes, they are both Feisty Fidos) offered by Lynn Medlin at Dog Town Dog Training.$^\Delta$

Patricia McConnell developed the Feisty Fido program for reactive dogs. Her book, "Feisty Fido,"△ will teach you how to get great results, even if you have a reactive dog.

If you have a Feisty Fido and can find a Feisty Fido class in your area, I highly recommend the experience.

When pet parents who are frustrated by certain behaviors commit to their dog's training, the result is marked improvement and reduced frustration for both the dog and humans. Note the word "commit." Make sure you know your tolerance level before adopting a certain dog and whether his specific behavioral issues (if he has any) will be a problem for you. Sometimes dogs develop issues unexpectedly, but the good news is that there are many resources to help.

Jody Miller-Young committed to training her newly adopted dog, and after consistent training, behavior modification and ultimately a move, she is happy to say that it was all worth it. You can read about it in her blog Bark and Swagger.△

## In-Home Private Training

Some families prefer to have a trainer come to their home. Many rescue organizations offer a few free training sessions with a staff trainer to help you get started.

*"I am a dog trainer, but actually, I am a people trainer. I do this because I want dogs to have a better life. If I train the owners, then the dogs will have a better life. Just today I got an email and a picture of one of my clients that really confirmed I am doing something positive. My first contact with this woman was a phone call wherein she was crying because she just adopted a dog from the SPCA and felt it was a big mistake. I hung up the phone and immediately drove to her house. After four visits with her and her*

*family, they are now in love with this dog and he is a part of their family. The photo she sent me is of her and the dog in a kayak together and she said, '…this is all because of you, or he would have gone back to the SPCA.' I am so glad that I can do my part on my pin-sized spot on the planet."*

—Leah Hutchison Pacitto, Owner,
Dog Gone Good Dog Training
www.doggonegooddogtraining.com

## Exercise and Socialization

A properly exercised dog is a happy dog. Discerning your dog's physical ability by taking into account his age, size and temperament is a good way to figure out the best form of exercise for him. Be sure to check with your vet before starting a new exercise regimen. Some dogs really are lap dogs and require minimal exercise. Others are high energy, young or have working breed blood (like herding breeds, hounds or retrievers) and require more exercise or even a job! Some dogs are Frisbee dogs, or dock diving dogs or show dogs. Many dogs fall somewhere in between incredibly athletic and couch potato. Some simply require daily walks, and a ball thrown to them for a few minutes in your yard.

*"When you do fun activities with your dog, you come to respect and understand each other better. There is a difference between taking your dog for a walk where you are on the phone and neither one of you is paying attention to the other and taking your dog to a fun activity where you are communicating the entire time. Incorporating obedience training into any fitness training makes your dog think and shows him that you are paying attention. It also establishes the alpha position making your dog more relaxed and better behaved. This comes in handy while doing any fitness related*

*activity where you need good communication and a well-behaved dog. Dogs don't care what you wear, how you look or how fast you are—as long as they are with you, they are happy!"*
—Dawn Celapino, Founder, Leash Your Fitness
www.leashyourfitness.com

Consider the weather when planning your dog's exercise regimen. In the summer, exercise him early in the day before it gets too hot, and only bring him out for a limited time in winter if he can't handle cold temperatures. Be sure to protect his paws and pads from extreme conditions. If you notice your dog limping or not using his paw or leg, it may be something simple like a burr stuck in his pad, which you can easily remove. If any limping persists, take him to the veterinarian to get checked out.

Foxtails are another potential walking hazard, especially in the Western US. To learn more about what they look like and signs that your dog might have picked one up, visit the Dogington Post article "What Every Dog Owner Should Know About Foxtails."△

## Walks

Daily walks are a great exercise and bonding opportunity for you and your dog. Plus it helps your dog burn off excess energy that could otherwise lead to destructive behavior in your home.

The benefits of walking dogs are much needed exercise (for both of you!), a chance for your dog to learn his new neighborhood and surroundings, and meeting other dogs if you wish to socialize your dog with other dogs in the neighborhood.

Many people tend to carry their purse-sized dogs. That's fine sometimes, but be sure to let their feet touch the ground regularly to keep their bodies strong.

My medium and large-sized dogs are walked two to three times daily, with at least one walk long enough to tire them out. That can be as short as 20 minutes, but when I have time I like to walk them for longer than 30 minutes. Some dogs only need a few short walks, but every dog needs to be exercised. I use our walks as an opportunity to reinforce their training by carrying treats with me and rewarding them for positive behaviors, like waiting at a corner or just doing a "watch me" command to keep them focused on me.

Ninja and Gonzo are dog reactive. Gonzo doesn't really care about other dogs unless we attempt to meet them, at which point he becomes aggressive. Ninja wants to meet every single dog he sees and generally loves them, but if they exhibit fear or aggression, he will react. So for the most part, to be safe, we avoid interacting with other dogs during our walks.

## Walking Safety and Etiquette

Before we go out for a walk, I grab a bunch of dog poop bags and fill a small plastic baggie with treats, which I use as training rewards. I make sure my dogs' leashes and head collars are securely on before I open the door. Other dogs walking in front of the house make my dogs crazy. (They are very protective of their domain and family.) I always peek out to see if anyone is coming before I open the door.

You can learn more about loose leash walking from Petfinder.com's article "I Pull, You Pull."[Δ]

Our dog T-bone hated skateboards and motorcycles. I recently learned that the sound they make may sound like a growl to a dog! I had no idea my dog thought the neighborhood kids on skateboards were growling at him! Every time we encountered one he went berserk. My goal was to see or hear them before he did so I could keep him calm. It usually worked but not all the time. If your dog has a really persistent fear, you can try desensitizing training with the guidance of a professional trainer.

Other potential hazards on the walk are dogs running alongside their pet parent, bicycles, kids running past, and other small animals.

The trick is to be hyper-vigilant when walking your dog so that you see any of these distractions before he does. It is impossible to be attentive when you are also on your phone, so leave it in your pocket and make dog walking time quality time.

JJ, our first dog, wanted to meet every dog we encountered. I learned, however, that not every dog wanted to meet JJ. It is important to ask the other dog parent if it's OK for your dogs to check each other out. Until you know your dog well, let your neighbors with dogs know that you don't know how your dog will react.

If you live near a beach or other open space where other dogs might be, be mindful of leash laws and whether it is legal for your dog to be on that hiking trail, park, or beach either on-leash or off-leash.

*"Squirrel!!!"*

## Exercise Classes With Your Dog

A trend taking off around the US is exercise classes with your dog.

*"Your dog will behave much better when he is mentally stimulated and exercised until he is tired. You can find activities that incorporate hiking, surfing, SUPing, kayaking, camping, yoga, trail running, and boot camp classes **ALL WITH YOUR DOG!**"*
—Dawn Celapino, Founder, Leash Your Fitness
www.leashyourfitness.com

Additionally, K9 Fit Clubs®, "health, fitness and wellness for both dogs and people," are popping up all over the country.

*"Created by veterinarians, personal trainers, doctors, and animal behaviorists, our programs are scientifically based [and] reach the entire bell curve of fitness for both people and their dogs."*
—Tricia Montgomery, Founder, K9 Fit Club
K9fitclub.com

You can check the K9 Fit Club△ website to see if there's one near you.

## Hikes

Hiking is also a great supplement to daily walks in your neighborhood. Hiking exposes you and your dog to challenging new terrain and fresh air. Be aware, however, of the potential dangers of excessive heat, dehydration, terrain that is hard on paws and snakes or other dangerous creatures. Your vet can provide rattlesnake vaccinations if need be which can allow you some extra lifesaving time as you get to the vet for treatment. Dawn Celapino of Leash Your Fitness created a handy hiking reference guide PDF[Δ] and our friends at PetHub.com and Go Pet Friendly.com created an infographic offering tips for dog-friendly hiking.[Δ]

## Running Your Dog

Are you a runner? Perhaps you have an athletic dog who loves running. Or he's super high energy and you ride your bicycle with him running alongside. For some people and dogs this is great. But how often do you see dogs trailing behind the bike struggling to keep up?

Be sure to constantly assess your dog's fitness, taking into account his age and mobility. According to Dr. Jessica Waldman, VMD, CVA, CCRT of California Animal Rehabilitation (CARE)[Δ], dogs should probably not run for exercise past the age of four.

What's your favorite way to exercise or spend time with your dog?

## Dog Parks

Dog parks were created so that dogs can run off leash in a public but enclosed environment. Some people love dog parks and they work great for their family. The dog gets to run around and be social and it is an opportunity for you to be social too. We used to take our dogs to the dog park and they were always tuckered out afterwards. There is something very freeing for a dog to be able to run around off leash.

Be aware, though, that there are a few drawbacks to dog parks.

1. Some dogs do tend to fight. Whether it's over a toy, a snack or just because some dogs don't like each other, it happens. Your

dog could potentially end up in a fight even if he is not usually the aggressor. It is frightening when it happens.

2. There is also a greater chance of your dog contracting a disease at a dog park from things like communal water bowls and shared toys.

3. Plus, they come back smelly and filthy from the park. So if you take your dog to the park, plan to give him a bath afterwards.

Before attempting the dog park, I suggest getting a good sense of his temperament, fears, and his ability to interact with other dogs by walking him in your neighborhood. Let him get to know all the sights and smells of his surroundings while settling in with you as his new dog parent. Then check out the dog park if that is still interesting to you.

In Module 5, I invite you to explore a healthy lifelong relationship with your dog, and more about adopting senior and special needs dogs.

# MODULE 5

# ADVANCED DOG PARENTING

*"And the fox said to the little prince: men have forgotten this truth, but you must not forget it. You become responsible, forever, for what you have tamed."*

—Antoine de Saint-Exupery

## PART I

## LIVING YOUR NEW LIFE

IN THIS FINAL MODULE, I show you how to cultivate a fun and nurturing long-term relationship with your dog along with advanced pet parenting guidance.

### While You Are Away From Home

Perhaps you have a lot of love to give but also have a busy schedule. In fact, your busy schedule might be a reason why you weren't ready to adopt a dog until now. Many potentially wonderful pet parents have full time jobs and choose not to adopt because they can't give a dog the attention he needs. In some cases this is best for both parties.

But there are great solutions that allow you to give a deserving dog a loving home even if you have a full-time job outside of the home. Quality doggie daycare is one option. Alternatively, pet sitters and dog walkers visit or stay in your home (if you are traveling) making sure your dog is well exercised, socialized and attended to during the day.

**Pet Sitters**:

We choose to have a trusted pet sitter stay with our dogs in our home when we travel. We used to have friends and family stay, but our dogs are a challenge, requiring professional care. I met Nicole Gallardo of Fido Fun Walks[Δ] in LA at a dog training class and another friend hired her first, so I completely trusted her when she started taking care of my dogs. Be sure to choose someone who comes recommended, has references and/or you already know and trust.

Nicole, our super awesome pet sitter, is great about walking or playing with my dogs and often brings her totally chill dog Porter along. My dogs love Porter and think of him as another brother. You may prefer that your pet sitter not bring her dog around (and your pet sitter should be accommodating) but for us, it's a bonus! Nicole is also our dog walker for the days that I'm too busy to give them the exercise they require.

*"Pet-parents are becoming increasingly educated on their care options and investing more time in selecting the best care possible for their beloved pets. In the past, many have relied on the 'kid down the street' or friends to take care of their pets while they are out of town or working—but we are now seeing a more discriminating pet owner. The pet owners we hear from are doing their research—and they want pet-care providers who are trained, background*

*checked and insured. At the end of the day, we all want the best possible care for our pets (who are our family) and as more and more pet owners become aware of professional options, they are taking advantage."*

—Beth Stultz, Director of Marketing & Education,
Pet Sitters International
www.petsit.com

If you are looking for professional pet sitters in your area please check out Pet Sitters International.<sup>Δ</sup>

What information should you share with your pet sitter? PetHub.com and GoPetFriendly.com give you ideas in their infographic, "Preparing for the Pet Sitter."<sup>Δ</sup>

**Doggie Daycare:**
Some dogs need human supervision for many hours while you work, and doggie daycare offers the bonus of socialization. There are more and more doggie daycare facilities popping up everywhere to meet the demand. Some offer grooming, training and other services, while others simply offer supervision in a playgroup setting. Be sure to learn about the reputation of the facility that interests you.

*"Grace spent the first year of her life in a shelter, after being abandoned twice. I thought she'd be happy to have a home, and she was. But she had a hard time trusting people. Once I realized that her 'safe space' was around other dogs, we started going to doggie daycare twice a week to hang out with her pals. Her 'job' there is to find the new dogs, the shy dogs, the scared dogs, and take them under her wing. She's brilliant at it—it is her gift born from hardship. Through it, she has risen above her own fears,*

*and taught all who know her about the instinctive compassion of dogs."*

—Beth Larsen, Founder, Waggletops

www.waggletops.com

**Boarding**:

If you travel, and choose not to utilize a pet sitter, consider boarding your dog at a well-reputed doggie hotel. I love my veterinarian and they offer boarding, but they don't walk the dogs for liability reasons. Some families feel comfortable boarding at their vet, but check with yours to make sure your dog will get proper attention. Your new family member deserves to have fun or at least some reasonable stimulation while you travel and cooping them up all day can be traumatizing.

Years ago, our dog Emma chewed her way out of the private room we had gotten for her in a boarding facility and was ultimately demoted to the kennel. Oops. My friends, Leslie and Paul, have had much better success with boarding. Their dog Whistler loves staying at Topanga Pet Resort where he enjoys an open rural play experience. They also love Wags Doggie Hotel in Los Angeles.

For a complete list of reputable doggie accommodations and services, check out Pet-Service-Directory.com. You will find listings for: Pet Sitters, Dog Walkers, Pet Boarding, Dog Training, Pet Grooming, Pet Waste Removal and Doggie Daycare.

Or ask around for recommended dog boarding from friends you trust. Never leave your dog home alone for extended periods of time or overnight in case there is an emergency.

*"Your precious pooch will need plenty of play time and socialization, especially with other furry friends! As pet parents and pet care services industry entrepreneurs ourselves, we are huge advocates of providing your beloved furry family members the opportunity to*

*participate in stimulating activities like daycare, playgroups and training activities while boarding at their favorite pet resorts. This will help keep your pups active, well-socialized and safe while having fun!"*

—Amber Kirsten-Smit & Andy Smit,
Co-Founders, SwiftPet™, Inc.
www.swiftpet.com

**Separation Anxiety:**

A lot of dogs experience intense stress when their owners leave home even for just a few minutes. This usually manifests itself through any number of destructive behaviors, such as chewing furniture legs, opening cabinets, pulling out garbage and leaving it strewn everywhere, shredding stuffing from pillows, and lots of barking and whining (all of which I've experienced with my own dogs). This behavior is commonly referred to as "separation anxiety."

The good news is, separation anxiety can be helped with a little training. Just remember to be patient while your dog is adjusting to your home. Avoid buying new furniture and remember to keep your shoes, socks and other potentially off-limits goods out of harms way. Never be afraid to seek help from a professional trainer or behaviorist. They can offer lots of great ideas for your particular situation. In addition to a pet sitter, there are other ways to distract and entertain your pup while you are out.

Adopt-a-Pet.com offers an article with tips to prepare your dog for success when you can't watch and entertain him called "Help Your Dog Stop Crying When Left Alone."[Δ] And if you believe your dog is counter surfing while you are out or even while you are at home, Adopt-a-Pet's blog "How to Keep a Dog Off Kitchen Counters"[Δ] might help.

In combating separation anxiety, I can't stress enough how important it is for your dog to be well exercised. The separation anxiety article above also suggests having a buddy for your dog.

I highly recommend adopting two dogs! Maybe not at the same time, but (in my experience) it's *not* twice the work and they have a buddy when you aren't home. My dogs get a long exercise walk in the morning but inevitably need another short one mid to late morning, which is all it takes for them to settle down. With a little time you'll get to know your dog's needs.

Dog TV$^\Delta$ is another tool to help alleviate your dog's anxiety. Using technology, Dog TV allows you to choose content that provides relaxation, stimulation or exposure (to special sounds and visuals) for your dog while you are out. TV, of course, is no substitute for having you there, but in a pinch it could make all the difference!

Increasingly, offices are becoming dog friendly too, so ask your company if you can bring your dog to work with you!

Does your dog exhibit naughty behavior when you are out? Or even while you are in the house? I'd love to hear your stories and how you remedied the behavior!

## Traveling With Your Dog

If you wish to take your dog along with your family on vacation, consult: GoPetFriendly.com$^\Delta$ or PetsWelcome.com$^\Delta$ first. You will find tons of dog-friendly resources including hotels, air travel; lodging and attractions. If you are traveling out of state with your dog, familiarize yourself with state regulations and be sure to have a Certificate of Veterinary Inspection (also referred to as Official Health Certificates or Health Certificates) for any state that requires you to travel with one.

**Flying**:

I've never taken my dogs on flights with me, partly because I haven't gone anywhere long enough to warrant it and partly because I would hate for them to be in the cargo section unnecessarily. Small dogs may travel with you under your seat if they are small enough to fit in an approved carrier. Be sure they have plenty of room to turn around in the carrier and consider potty issues on longer flights.

**Driving**:

How often do you see people driving with a dog on their lap? The distraction is as dangerous as texting and in some states it is illegal to drive with an unrestrained pet.

- Some people use crates for car rides, or their dogs are behind bars in the back of an SUV or hatchback. Either method will keep your dog from roaming around the car and distracting you, but unless they are restrained, they can get seriously injured or injure someone else in a crash.

- There are now pet restraint systems so your dog can ride more safely in the car with you. Sleepypod's Clickit[Δ] system has excellent crash ratings for medium to larger dogs. If you have a smaller dog, you can check out the Pupsaver.[Δ]

- I just recently purchased the Clickit system for my dogs and it's pretty easy to use. I recommend adjusting the harness before you actually need to take your dog in the car so you aren't fumbling with it (like I was!) when it's time to leave. Dogs should never ride in the back of a pickup truck even if they are on a leash.

**Out on the Town:**

Many families like having their dogs with them all the time and take them everywhere. Restaurants are becoming increasingly dog friendly, especially those with outdoor seating. In some towns, like Portland, there are dog bowls with fresh water everywhere. For a list of pet friendly restaurants nationwide, check out PetFriendlyRestaurants. com.[Δ]

# MODULE 5 PART II

# ADVANCED TRAINING AND SPECIAL CERTIFICATIONS

BEYOND BASIC TRAINING (MODULES 3 AND 4), there is so much more you can do with your dog for his stimulation, improving behavior and strengthening your bond.

## Canine Good Citizen Designation

After basic training, many pet parents choose to obtain the Canine Good Citizen® designation for their dog, which requires more advanced training. From the American Kennel Club (AKC®) website:

*"Started in 1989, the CGC Program is designed to reward dogs who have good manners both at home and in the community. The Canine Good Citizen® Program is a two-part program that stresses responsible pet ownership for owners and basic good manners for dogs. Many dog owners choose Canine Good Citizen® training as the first step in training their dogs. As you work with your dog to teach the CGC skills, you'll discover the many benefits and joys of training. Training will enhance the bond between you and your dog. Dogs who have a solid obedience education are a joy to live with. They respond well to household routines, have good manners in the presence of people and other dogs and they fully enjoy the*

*company of the owner who took the time to provide training, intellectual stimulation and a high quality life.*"

To read more about the CGC Program,^Δ^ please visit the AKC® website. Please note that the CGC Program is not exclusive to AKC papered dogs. Mixed breeds and rescued dogs are welcome to participate as well. JJ and T-bone were as mixed bred as you can get and they were both CGC certified.

Even dogs rescued from a notorious dog-fighting ring were eventually able to become CGC Certified. You may remember the Michael Vick dog-fighting story from 2007. When the ring was broken up, many of the dogs were adopted by highly skilled and loving rehabilitation organizations, attempting to offer these abused dogs a higher quality of life. Best Friends Animal Society rescued 22 of those dogs. The court required that some of the dogs formerly involved in the Michael Vick ring obtain a Canine Good Citizen designation as a prerequisite for adoption from Best Friends Animal Society. Others of the dogs at Best Friends were allowed to be adopted with the proviso that they continued working towards CGC certification with an approved trainer in their family's homes. The rest are at Best Friends and are "healing and blossoming, enjoying comfort and companionship here among the red rock canyons."^Δ^

You can learn more about the "Vicktory Dogs"^Δ^ as well as the incredible work Best Friends^Δ^ does for more than 1700 animals at their sanctuary and beyond.

## Service and Therapy Dogs

It is increasingly common to see dogs with Service Dog vests. Those dogs are working and it is prudent to ask the handler whether their dog can be approached or petted.

Many people are only familiar with service dogs that help the visually impaired, but there are now specially trained service dogs available for a wide variety of challenges. For example, service dogs can help alert their person to oncoming seizures, or warn of danger due to peanut allergies! There are also service dogs who help with emotional issues, such as Post Traumatic Stress Disorder.

Traditionally, service dogs are specially trained from puppyhood. While many service dogs are still pure bred, there are wonderful programs like Freedom Service Dogs[Δ] that rescue shelter dogs and custom train them to address a specific need. I mention this to reinforce the idea that any breed, mixed or not, puppy or adult, can be trained to be of service, EVEN IF THEY CAME FROM THE SHELTER! Of course the organizations that choose and train service dogs have experience with the necessary traits the dogs must possess in order to be successful.

Shelter dogs who were relinquished for poor behavior even learned how to drive. Check out the video link on my website of dogs in New Zealand actually driving a car!

## Animal Assisted Therapy

Years ago I was hospitalized for pneumonia and not showing any signs of improvement. About four days into my stay, a woman peeked her head into my room, knocked on the door and asked if I'd like a visit from a dog.

I looked up from my fog and said "A dog? Of course!"

She spread a clean sheet on my bed, the dog jumped up and I petted him and chatted with the woman for a few minutes. It was lovely!

While it didn't take the place of being with my own dogs, I was thrilled to have had the visit. Needless to say, I turned the corner the next day. Was it the new medicine or the dog visit? Maybe both. All I know is it was a great experience that lifted my spirits.

The dog that came to see me was an Animal Assisted Therapy Dog. If you are interested in being an animal assisted therapy team with your dog in a therapeutic setting (hospitals, schools, nursing homes and mental health institutions are just a few examples), it's a good idea to start with the Canine Good Citizen designation (though not required). From there you will get a sense of your dog's temperament and whether this could be a fit.

Petpartners.org[Δ] shares that "The Therapy Animal Program demonstrates that positive human-animal interventions improve the physical, emotional and psychological lives of those we serve." They also explain that becoming a team is not as much about dog training the animal as it is the handler. "The key to safe and effective visits is the training for the 'human end of the leash'."[Δ]

> *"Joey has CGC certification. We did that for the challenge of the training. He's a shy dog and many of the requirements of [the training] were things that helped him be more comfortable in society. Because he is shy and not very trusting of people, he would NOT be a good candidate for being a therapy dog."*
> —Jeannette Hartman, Fido Universe
> www.fidouniverse.com

I have a lot of respect for Jeannette and her awareness that her dog wouldn't be a suitable therapy dog.

Assuming you are comfortable in moving forward as a therapy team, here's how it works: You will attend a series of classes together until you become certified. From there, you, along with the organization determine where your therapy team would be best utilized. There are organizations around the country that certify Animal Assisted Therapy teams. The Good Dog Foundation$^\Delta$ is highly regarded on the East Coast. Pet Partners$^\Delta$ is nationally recognized and can help certify a team all over the country.

> *"Sophie and I chose PetPartners.org (previously known as the Delta program), one of the oldest and largest. We took a 6-week course at the Bideawee Animal Shelter$^\Delta$ in NYC and learned how to work as a team to familiarize Sophie with the kinds of things she might encounter in a nursing home or hospital, like wheelchairs, walkers and unexpected noises and actions. She also learned how to ignore things she found on the floor. At our final evaluation, we were able to demonstrate what we learned in all of the various situations created for us. I also passed a written exam. The certification lasted 2 years.*
>
> *A feisty, fun-loving and social little dog, Sophie has made our lives infinitely richer. We now visit an adult day care center and a school for severely disabled children each week. She thrives during those visits, calmly letting people pet her, brush her and kiss her, and yes, throw fun toys and give her lots of treats!"*
>
> Jody Miller-Young, Bark & Swagger
> www.barkandswagger.com

## Reading Programs

Many schools now offer reading programs where children read to a visiting therapy dog. Often those dogs are therapy pets due to their calm manner and ability to sit still for extended periods of time. The dog is nonjudgmental and the child feels a sense of pride and mastery reading out loud rather than in a classroom situation where they might be mocked by their peers. Ultimately your pet must "want" to do this kind of work. You'll know if it's right for both of you. There are many local organizations that specialize in therapy dogs in reading programs. Dogs on Call$^\Delta$ is one example.

## Advanced Bonding Activities

In Module 4 we discussed exercise and training basics. In addition to the basics, there are a plethora of exciting alternate activities to challenge and engage your pup. High energy or working breeds will love the additional stimulation.

**Agility Classes**:
If you have a high-energy dog, an agility class (obstacle courses) could be perfect for him. People attend agility class with their dog for fun and exercise and some even compete with their dogs in competitions. Chances are you won't be ready for agility classes when you first bring your new dog home, but it is something to consider once he's comfortable and appears to be athletic. It is recommended that very young dogs and dogs at risk of orthopedic injuries avoid more strenuous activities.

*"Sophie has trained at agility, a strong sport for Podengos. We took three six-week agility courses at Animal Haven$^\Delta$ in NYC. They offer classes on an ongoing basis."*
—Jody Miller-Young, Bark & Swagger
www.barkandswagger.com

For more information visit The US Dog Agility Association.$^\Delta$

*"Go On Bella. Good Girl!"*

**Nose Work:**

Some dogs (and their owners) enjoy doing nose work—a great "job" for certain breeds, plus it's another opportunity to bond with your dog.

According to the K9 Nose Work® website:[Δ]

"Inspired by working detection dogs, K9 Nose Work is the fun search and scenting activity for virtually all dogs and people. This easy to learn activity and sport builds confidence and focus in many dogs, and provides a safe way to keep dogs fit and healthy through mental and physical exercise."

*"We adopted Dino just a few months ago. Since he's around 2 or 3 years old, not a puppy, we wanted to create as many opportunities to bond with him as possible. We've already taken him to two*

*obedience classes and just started doing nose work. I don't think nose work is generally popular for Boxers, but it definitely added something new to bond over and he seems to really enjoy it."*

—Melissa and Mars Sandoval,
Dog Parents to Dino, the Rescued Boxer

Other popular activities and sports are dock-diving, show dog competition, Frisbee, and I recently learned about freestyle dancing! Do you and your dog already participate in an activity not mentioned here? If so, let me know!

# MODULE 5 PART III

# SPECIALTY HEALTH AND WELLNESS

WHILE MANY DOGS ARE HEALTHY until they are much older, accidents and illnesses do occur, and it is wise to be familiar with a variety of care options.

## Advanced Veterinary Care

Everyone should provide their dog with basic veterinary care including annual check ups and either immunizations or titering (see Module 3 for information on basic veterinary care). If your dog develops anything requiring more than routine veterinary care, there are now specialty vets in most metropolitan areas that concentrate in everything from dermatology, to orthopedic care, to cancer treatment and more. Some veterinarians now offer holistic care as well.

Here's a little bit more in-depth information about:
- Canine Rehabilitation
- Canine Cancer
- Holistic Alternatives

### Canine Rehabilitation:
What we refer to as "Physical Therapy" in the human world is called Rehabilitation Therapy in the animal world. Canine rehab has begun gaining popularity as its numerous benefits are consistently proven.

According to the American Veterinary Medical Association (AVMA),[Δ] "With animal rehabilitation services becoming increasingly commonplace, more and more clients are recognizing that physical therapy is not just for people but can also mean pain relief, increased mobility, and an improved quality of life for pets as well."

After my first dog JJ passed, my other dog T-bone and I would go for long walks to help relieve our sadness. Just two weeks later, he couldn't walk. He was a mature but healthy dog who seemingly out of the blue wouldn't use his back leg. After months of tests and awfulness, we found Dr. Jessica Waldman at California Animal Rehabiltation,[Δ] or CARE, in Los Angeles. Once it was determined that T-bone had an autoimmune disease attacking his joints, rendering him unable to walk, the team at CARE made a plan to rehabilitate him. They used a combination of manual therapy, hydrotherapy, strength training, acupuncture and supplements, which complemented the steroids he was also required to take. After four months of not walking, T-bone was able to walk again!

During the few months that T-bone wasn't walking, we needed a way to help him up and down the stairs and into the car. He was a 65-pound dog and carrying him wasn't an option for me. CARE introduced us to a few very helpful products for compromised dogs that we have since shared with friends who are in a similar position.

These are the products that we used:

- The first is a Help 'Em Up™[Δ] harness. It fits securely around your dog aiding you to lift him up. Some dogs who can't use their legs wear one all the time to go in and out of the house to potty. The way the handles are positioned made picking up T-bone more like a picking up a suitcase and it was manageable.
- The second tool is a ramp to help him get in and out of the car. It took a few tries coaxing him up the ramp with a treat, but once he got it, it was awesome. This was another lifesaver and

stores easily when not in use. The brand that we use is called Solvit.[△]

- The third is removable carpet treads[△] for our hardwood staircase. Hardwood floors can be difficult for dogs who are already unsteady and stairs were impossible for T-bone. Adding the treads made it much easier for him to get traction. Plus, they are removable (you just place them down and then when you want them off, they are easily lifted) so if you don't love the way they look, you can just use them when your dog is using the stairs.

You can find a Certified Canine Rehabilitation Therapist at the Canine Rehabilitation Institute.[△] Be sure a veterinarian supervises the Canine Rehabilitation Therapy program you choose.

My dogs Ninja and Gonzo have both had orthopedic issues requiring therapy at CARE and daily medication for pain and joint swelling. We are mindful of their exercise regimen (not too strenuous), no sports requiring that they jump up (like Frisbee even though it looks like so much fun) and we keep them at a healthy weight to minimize stress on their joints.

**Canine Cancer:**

Sadly, cancer is increasingly common in dogs. Many families whose dogs have cancer are choosing to treat them with similar treatments to those that humans might receive (chemotherapy and radiation). We chose to treat our dog T-bone who had a fairly aggressive cancer. It can get quite pricey so that is a big consideration. But for the most part, dogs don't have the same awful reactions to chemo that humans have.

Maggie Marton of OhMyDog blog,[△] writes about many dog related topics, but openly sharing her experience with cancer is poignant and full of heart.

If you are in Southern California, I highly recommend City of Angels for canine cancer treatment. For all veterinary specialists in or out of SoCal, please visit Vet Specialists[Δ] (vetspecialists.com).

Whichever treatment you seek, having pet insurance can potentially help you save thousands of dollars. (See the section below about pet insurance to learn more.)

**Holistic Medicine:**

Holistic medicine takes multiple aspects of health into account—body, mind, spirit, and emotions. A growing number of veterinarians are considering alternative (holistic) treatments to complement traditional treatments. Many dog trainers and behaviorists are familiar with them as well.

**How holistic care can be applied to physical health and emotional well-being:**

The treatment at California Animal Rehabilitation, for example, combines traditional veterinary care along with rehabilitation therapy as well as other therapies like acupuncture, massage and nutritional supplements. Any one of the treatments at CARE is excellent, and when combined, the results are incredible.

Oftentimes, when you bring a new dog into your home, he will need some adjusting to feel completely comfortable. You don't know each other so a little stress is natural. While there are extreme cases where a dog's stress requires medication like doggie Prozac®, there are also many natural alternatives (including aromatherapy and Thunder-Shirt®△) worth trying before going the drug route.

*"A dog's sense of smell is remarkably better than ours. They have 40 times more scent receptors than humans, allowing them to identify smells up to 10,000 times better. With their remarkable olfactory memory, a dog's world revolves around scent. This is why aroma-therapy is ideal for use with dogs. Calming sprays and massage or grooming products containing essential oils can be physically applied to provide comfort for dogs that are fretful during storms, fireworks, travel, competition, adoption, bath time, veterinary or kennel visits, and holidays. Calming sprays can help dogs with sep-aration anxiety relax and feel safe, due to the association of scent with a person of comfort and a reassuring touch."*

—Vicki Rae Thorne, Earth Heart® Inc.,
Creator of Canine Calm®
www.earthheartinc.com

Some dogs seem very well adjusted and then one day something happens that freaks them out, like a thunderstorm. There are products available like the ThunderShirt, which essentially swaddle your dog to help him feel more secure.

ThunderShirt isn't exclusive to thunderstorms and can be used for any kind of negative stimuli that upsets your dog. Again, some people love this product, and others find it does nothing. Ask your trainer or behaviorist if they think it could be helpful to you.

In her article entitled "Holistic Health for New Adoptees," Dr. Christina Chambreau, DVM offers five holistic methods to help achieve health and behavior goals: Reiki, Flower Essences, Tellington TTouch®, Acupressure, and Healing Touch for Animals. You can learn more about each modality in the full article available on my website^, or by contacting her at My Healthy Animals (christinachambreau.com).

Always ask your vet before trying any new medication whether it is homeopathic, "natural" or traditional.

The American Holistic Veterinary Medical Association (AHVMA)^ has a listing of holistic veterinarians you can search if you are interested in holistic remedies for your dog.

> *"There's something about my dog Sweet Pea that has touched me on a deeper level. I love her so much, that when I can't find a product to safely and naturally do whatever it is she needs, I create it and add it to my company's arsenal of natural remedies. So my dog has literally inspired my career path and my company's every move. She's so special, I hope everyone gets to find a canine soul mate in their lifetime."*
>
> —Elyse Horvath, Owner, Natural Paws
> www.naturalpaws.net

**Pet Insurance:**

Years ago I bought pet insurance and never used it, which was a good thing, but ultimately when our pets needed care, the level of treatment they needed was outside the scope of what insurance covered. This was years ago and pet insurance has since become more comprehensive.

> *"My service dog, Jake, required surgery, which cost me thousands of dollars. Because I had pet insurance, I didn't have to think twice*

*about whether I could afford the procedure. My insurance company returned about 80% of my initial outlay allowing me to feel comfortable that I could provide him with the best care possible. I can't recommend pet insurance enough."*

—Beke Lubeach, Owner of Dog Bone Marketing Solutions
www.dogbonemarketing.com

Beke's story convinced me of the importance of pet insurance and now that coverage is so much more comprehensive than in years past, I researched plans for my dogs. I do recommend investigating pet insurance since it covers many basics as well as some expensive medical issues, should you encounter any down the road. Be sure to learn what is and is not covered by the policy you seek. Consumers Advocate[Δ] lists the 10 best insurance companies of 2015 to help you choose one that's best for you.

## In Case of Emergency

### Pet CPR and First Aid:

Did you ever see the commercial where the fireman saves the life of a kitten he has just rescued from a smoke-filled building? Pet CPR is something you can learn too, just like we learn CPR for humans. Denise Fleck of Sunny-dog Ink[Δ] and Arden Moore of Pet First Aid 4 U[®Δ] both teach Pet CPR and First Aid Classes. I took Arden's mini intro class at a Blog Paws[Δ] conference and was inspired to take Denise's full class (near my home) to really learn the material. Arden's course is a veterinarian-approved national pet first aid program, and you can contact Denise to take her course online!

Both Arden and Denise offer a variety of books and Sunny-dog Ink also offers first aid kits and quick reference posters. I highly recommend taking a class. There is so much you can learn, even basic reminders like not leaving toothpicks or pennies around because they could be harmful or even lethal. You can download Denise's comprehensive "Pawparedness Checklist for your dog"△ from my website to have in case of an emergency.

*"Veterinarians are the experts, but most of us don't have one velcroed to our hip 24/7, so YOU must react quickly and effectively at the scene when injury or illness takes place. Knowing what to do during those first few moments can make a life-saving difference for the dog in your care.*

*If you know how to:*
- *stop bleeding and bandage a wound, you can prevent severe blood loss and keep infection at bay.*
- *reduce a pet's body temperature, you can prevent brain damage and death.*
- *alleviate choking, you can prevent an animal, from going unconscious.*
- *be the pump at the time the pet's heart goes into arrest, you can keep blood and oxygen flowing until you get to the Animal ER.*

*Pet first aid is by no means a replacement for veterinary care, but you could potentially help your vet to help your dog if you alleviate critical trauma. Together you and your veterinarian work as a team for the wellbeing of your pet."*

—Denise Fleck, Sunny-dog Ink
www.sunnydogink.com

*"I was caring for two Cairn Terriers when one of them started choking. I am so grateful I had taken Denise Fleck's Pet First-Aid Class just the day before. I quickly took appropriate action and a biscuit shot out of the dog's mouth. There is nothing quite as*

*rewarding as knowing I had saved the day for this helpless little dog, and her wagging tail and thankful licks let me know she felt the same way."*

—Tina Kenny, TLC Pet Sitting, LA Based Pet Sitter

Arden Moore recommends having a Pet First Aid App on your phone, which I recently downloaded. While the app is clear that it is no substitute for proper veterinary care, it does offer many potentially lifesaving tips for a variety of pet emergencies, and chances are you will always have your phone with you.

# EXCEPTIONAL DOGS

## Special Needs

SPECIAL NEEDS DOGS OFFER AS MUCH love as any other dog, no matter their challenges.

There are a variety of "special needs" you may encounter, from physical limitations, to health and emotional/psychological limitations. There are many people who have a soft spot in their heart for the true underdog and maybe you are one of them. Just as there are breed rescues devoted to almost every breed, there are also rescue groups devoted to special needs dogs.

An example is Special Needs Animal Rescue and Rehabilitation (SNARR).[△]

> *"This goes back to finding the right pet for your lifestyle, needs, your experience level, budget and what calls to you. Some people get a lot out of rehabilitating a dog. It's highly rewarding to see a dog come out of his shell or overcome an abusive or neglectful upbringing. For the wrong family, they focus on the extra work involved but for the right family, they just see the opportunity to help the dog."*
> —Leela Ruiz, Owner, Dog and House
> www.dogandhouse.com

## Physical Challenges

Many dogs function perfectly well with compromised limbs, whether they were born that way or had an accident or disease that required amputation. Some dogs only have use of three or even two legs but are otherwise healthy. You may have seen a dog with wheels or prosthetics. There are now canine prosthetics being created with 3D printers!

When my dogs were being treated at California Animal Rehabilitation (CARE), I witnessed a variety of physical challenges. The beauty I saw was the commitment of the pet parent to help make them as comfortable as possible by bringing them for physical therapy and acupuncture, especially knowing how beneficial it can be.

Some dogs are deaf, blind or have a chronic but controlled illness. Often these dogs will do just fine with or without accommodations.

I recently learned about a deaf woman adopting a deaf dog named Rosie from a shelter. The shelter had taught Rosie some basic sign language for her commands, but they needed to find the perfect forever home for her. Watching them connect was truly beautiful. Check out Deaf Dogs Rock[Δ] for more information and support in deaf dog adoption and care.

There are also helpful devices to accommodate sight-impaired dogs so they don't crash into furniture and hurt themselves at home. An example is Halos for Paws.[Δ]

## Emotional Challenges

Many rescued dogs are physically fine but they have been abused or neglected, and require special care. What they need is some time, love and patience and they will begin to trust humans again. The pet adoption organization may be able to help you understand why your new dog is skittish or reactive and how you can begin to help him heal.

Some organizations, like the ASPCA®, have programs that endeavor to rehabilitate dogs who have been abused and neglected, resulting in minimal socialization skills. The program is so successful, even with seemingly hopeless cases, that there is renewed promise for rehabilitating many, many animals. You can read more about "A Second Chance for Traumatized Dogs"[Δ] at dianerosesolomon.com/links.

Our newest dog Ninja had a pretty rough first couple of years before we knew him, spending most of his time chained up in a backyard, followed by bouncing around from shelter to foster to boarding. He had separation anxiety and needed to be placed in a home with another dog. It was just perfect that we had Gonzo who also needed a buddy. They've been best buddies since. He still has some separation anxiety and will sometimes counter surf as soon as I walk out the door if I'm not diligent about putting stuff away.

A more extreme example of psychological challenges, and one that deserves a lot of attention, is animals who have suffered in laboratories and been used for product experimentation. Animal testing is outdated and barbaric. First of all, the products that have "successful" outcomes on dogs (or other animals for that matter,) don't necessarily have successful outcomes on humans, due to the differences in our physiology. Secondly, there are modern, *effective* technological alternatives to animal testing. And thirdly—who are we to say that another sentient being deserves to suffer for the potential sake of human health, just because they don't have the same cognitive, verbal or manual dexterity skills as we do?

According to Beagle Freedom Project,[Δ]

"Nearly 70,000 dogs were used in labs in 2012 [and]106,000 people die annually from drugs tested safe on animals."

That model clearly doesn't work.

"Beagles are the most popular breed for lab use because of their friendly, docile, trusting, forgiving, people-pleasing personalities. The research industry says they adapt well to living in a cage and are inexpensive to feed."

Almost none of these dogs have ever lived anywhere but in a cage— they are bred specifically for laboratory use. I remember bawling while watching a Beagle Freedom/ARME video years ago in which Beagles are walking on grass for the very first time and didn't know what it was. The work that Beagle Freedom is doing to help these animals is unbelievable. While they work to find loving homes for these sweet dogs once they are released, they simultaneously encourage the public to purchase cruelty-free products via their Cruelty Cutter app.

Dogs who have been in captivity and have no social experience have their own set of needs. Many are unable to handle the crate environment. But they still enjoy that den-like experience. Here's how Leela Ruiz, a Beagle Freedom supporter, and owner of Dog and House got creative.

*"My 'hoodie' bed was inspired by dogs used for laboratory testing, to help them with their residual emotional and fear issues. My friend, author Teresa Rhyne, adopted a dog rescued from a laboratory by Beagle Freedom Project and asked me to design a custom bed for him. When she mentioned that he loved to burrow in blankets it made perfect sense to me, since a dog abused with experiments and caged for his whole life would have a love-hate relationship with confinement. Sadly the cage was both his security and abuser. Obviously you cannot use a traditional crate with a former laboratory animal, but what he was doing was creating his own safe place by burrowing. I created a design that allowed him the opportunity to self-soothe in the softest, most luxurious fabrics and cushioning*

*where he could come and go freely, turning it into a positive, comforting experience."*

—Leela Ruiz, Owner, Dog and House
www.dogandhouse.com

## Senior Dogs

Senior pets are wonderful because they are already past the needy and high-energy stage. They just want to be loved and love you back.

There's a children's book called *Let's Get a Pup Said Kate*, by Bob Graham in which a family goes to the shelter to find a puppy and next to the puppy kennel is a senior dog who catches their eye. But their mission was to bring home a puppy, which is what they do. Their hearts get the best of them and they return the next day to adopt the senior dog too.

Puppies are cute, and playful, there's no denying that. But there is something satisfying about adopting a senior dog who deserves to live the end of his life in a loving home.

Dogs are considered "senior" after seven years of age, depending on the breed. Smaller dogs generally live longer and some larger breeds like Great Danes and Boxers typically have shorter lifespans. Many senior dogs still have plenty of pep in their step, but if you are considering adopting a senior dog it's a good idea to ask your vet for some activity guidelines. There are many things you can do to help keep your dog comfortable as he ages including (but not limited to) cutting back on strenuous exercise (if warranted), adding supplements to his diet, and possibly adding canine rehabilitation (either administered at a facility or possibly through a supervised home program of stretching and strengthening).

*"Pets age much faster than we expect. It is very important to constantly evaluate their enthusiasm for each activity. If your pet runs with you, plays fetch, goes to the dog park or does long walks, do you notice that his ability or interest in the duration of these activities has altered? Did your pet historically want to fetch for hours and now only does a few jaunts before they become tired? Does your pet begin leash walks in front of you and by the end they are behind you? If your pet is sleeping for several hours or longer after intense activity, they are likely sore. Behavior changes may indicate pain and also intolerance as they age, so try to be proactive and adjust his activities. A rehabilitation certified veterinarian can evaluate your pet and help you to determine what exercise is appropriate as your pet ages."*

—Dr. Jessica Waldman, VMD, CVA, CCRT,
California Animal Rehab (CARE)
www.calanimalrehab.com

This next story is excerpted from "The Love of a Dog: The Story of Sushi" by Denise Fleck. For the complete story, please visit my website.

*"This woman led the Akita to my car, patted her head and proclaimed she'd miss her 'almost as much as her rose bushes.' The woman was moving in two days and had made no plans to find a home for her dog. She had called the pound to have 'Sushi' picked up assuming she would immediately be adopted, but with the number of homeless animals in Los Angeles, reality is a much different picture, and for an 8-year-old Japanese Akita...reality would be grim. My yellow Labrador 'Sunny' whom my husband Paul and I rescued from her 'last day' at a shelter 9 years earlier had recently passed away. I wasn't ready to become attached to another dog, yet my heart made me get involved and adopt Sushi. Sushi*

*went with us for walks, car rides, enjoyed breakfasts at pet-friendly cafés, and entertained herself with her first ever toy! At night she slept on her own bed next to ours with what was unmistakably a smile. How could we ever imagine life without her? Over the next four years, the graying of her face softened her look, but a more profound transformation was the inner beauty that blossomed through her eyes.*

*At the age of 12 ½ Sushi joined Sunny on 'The Rainbow Bridge.' Although it is painful to say good-bye, the memories will forever be cherished, as we are confident Sushi's time with us was lived to the fullest. Sushi helped me understand that I could find more than one soul mate canine companion. True, your time together may be short when adopting a senior, but the quality of that time far outweighs the quantity of years. Loving Sushi and being loved by her truly changed my life and led me on my path of adopting seniors and spreading the word about how amazing they really are."*

—Denise Fleck, Sunny-dog Ink,
*The Love of A Dog: The Story of Sushi*

*"Blessed is the person who has earned the love of an old dog."*
—Sydney Jeanne Seward

So what can you expect when you adopt a dog? Adopting a dog and saving a life is so rewarding, but that's only the beginning. The constant companionship and unconditional love from your pet is unparalleled, no matter their age, breed, size or where they came from.

# REHOMING AS A LAST RESORT

SOMEONE RECENTLY ASKED ME WHAT to do when you *know* that your dog isn't good with kids. She was pregnant and sure she was going to have to rehome her beloved dog. Another friend recently got married and her husband's family was highly allergic to her pets. While I advocate doing everything you can to keep your dog in your home, sometimes rehoming is the most humane choice.

Before doing anything, check your adoption contract because many rescue groups require that you return the dog to that organization rather than placing him yourself. Rehoming is heartbreaking, but if you don't have a contract and you've already worked with a trainer, behaviorist and veterinarian then it is probably best to find a loving home for your dog. You should do a lot of research and find a suitable home, perhaps with a friend or a family member.

Remember that bringing a dog to a shelter doesn't mean that they will find a good home. In many shelters when they are overcrowded and the dogs' time is up, time is up. I know I would feel terrible giving up a family member and not knowing that he was safe and happy. And please, never place an ad either in your local newspaper or online as your beloved dog may get "adopted" by someone with unscrupulous intentions.

As a last resort, Adopt-a-Pet.com's article "How Can I Find a New Home for My Pet"[Δ] may be helpful.

# SAYING GOODBYE

*"If there are no dogs in Heaven, then when I die I want to go where they went."*

—Will Rogers

MANY PEOPLE HAVE TOLD ME they don't want to adopt a dog because a dog's life is so short and it's too heartbreaking when they pass. While never adopting a dog will protect you from that inevitable feeling of loss, the experience of unconditional love between you and your dog is more than worth it.

It is sad but true that our pets don't live nearly as long as we'd like. Hopefully they will go comfortably and quietly in the middle of the night, but often that just isn't the case. And sometimes, they die quite unexpectedly, which can be traumatic.

If your dog is very sick, there is specialty veterinary medicine that can potentially prolong your dog's life. Whether you choose to treat your dog's serious illness will depend on many factors. We decided against treating our dog JJ's cancer because he had so many other health issues, there was a good chance he wouldn't survive the treatment. We just made sure he was happy and comfortable for as long as possible.

We did, however, choose to treat T-bone's cancer because he was an otherwise healthy dog and the treatment seemed viable. It was a huge expense because we didn't have pet insurance at the time. The treatment worked somewhat in keeping him comfortable, but it did not extend his life as long as we had hoped.

Ultimately, we knew that when our dogs stopped enjoying food and appeared extremely uncomfortable, the compassionate choice was to let them go. We chose to humanely euthanize them so as not to prolong their suffering.

Saying goodbye to each of my dogs was among the saddest experiences I have had. I remember asking my vet how I would know when it was the right time. She told me that I wouldn't really know the exact time and that many people end up beating themselves up over it. She said if you euthanize your dog before you truly believe his enjoyment of life is over, you may feel like you did it too soon. But, if you know deep down you are holding on because you can't bear to say goodbye, you may regret making him suffer longer than necessary. It is a personal decision so just use your best judgment.

*"I've had this heartbreaking experience a few (too many) times in the last five years. Right or wrong, the way I decided was by identifying their five or so favorite things— food, walks, laying in the sun, seeing certain people. When they were no longer interested in 4 of those things, I planned the best possible 'last best day'. Then it was time."*

—Sara Henderson, Chief Foodie, BOGO Bowl
www.bogobowl.com

There are many resources available to help you through the grieving process including, pet grief books, counselors and groups. You can also memorialize your dog in a way that speaks to you, including writing about them or using lovely products like the BioUrn® (explained below).

When it was time to say goodbye to JJ, our first dog, we went to the veterinarian office where he could be humanely euthanized. I held him in my lap as we gently said goodbye. We clipped a piece of soft fur from behind JJ's ears before we left. I don't have words to express how difficult the process was.

I arrived home from the vet that morning and there was a package waiting on my doorstep. My dear friend Kerri had gone to the bookstore as soon as it opened and picked up a copy of Cynthia Rylant's book *Dog Heaven,* ostensibly for my kids. They enjoyed it, but I think I got a little more out of the book than they did. This gesture from a friend meant a lot to me and helped ease my pain.

Soon after we said goodbye to JJ, I learned of in-home euthanasia, which I now recommend. We found Dr. Michelle Lorenzen, of Choice Veterinary Care[Δ] an incredible Los Angeles-based vet who did home visits and was available 24/7. Dogs are usually terrified at the vet's office, so it made complete sense to have her come to us.

Of course this is a personal process, but Dr. Lorenzen really helped us. I had called her in advance when our dog T-bone was beginning his decline. She assured me that she would be available in an emergency situation and that I was welcome to call and ask questions anytime.

The final morning that we called Dr. Lorenzen, T-bone couldn't stand up and he wouldn't eat. She and her assistant assessed our lovely boy and agreed it was obvious that it was his time. We decided not to have our kids present because we felt they were too young. Whether your kids participate should be a family decision. We did include them in our discussions about his passing before and after and encouraged them to share any feelings that came up.

Dr. Lorenzen suggested that Gonzo, our other dog, be in a different room so we could give our full attention to T-bone while we said goodbye. They helped T-bone onto a blanket on my lap with my husband by my side. While they did their preparation, we told him how much we loved him, what a good boy he was and petted, and snuggled him. When he was gone, we were allowed to take as much time with him as needed. We clipped a piece of fur from him, just like we did with JJ. The tears flowed then and they flow now as I write this. There is no easy way to say goodbye to a family member, including the furry ones. Gonzo was then allowed to see T-bone so that he could recognize that T-bone was gone.

We decided to have T-bone cremated by himself (as opposed to in a group cremation). While we waited for his ashes to be returned to us, Dr. Lorenzen made a donation in T-bone's name to a wonderful organization called HOPE.ᐃ HOPE provides full service veterinary care to pets of homeless people in Los Angeles. When we received his ashes, we also received a loving note from Dr. Lorenzen as well as T-bone's paw print in a ceramic tile. She made the whole experience much more bearable for us, and I hope for T-bone as well.

*"When a beloved pet is aging, ill or has died, your feelings of grief can be overwhelming. Your feelings are perfectly normal and you don't need to face this alone! Pet grief counselors are skilled at helping you ease your pain and find peace."*
—Judy Helm Wright, Pet Grief Coach, Death of My Pet
www.deathofmypet.com

When JJ and T-bone passed, I wrote them letters. I wanted to remember their mannerisms and quirks because I knew that over time my memory would fade. I also have a little shrine for them in my closet. Their ashes are seated on one of their soft beds, alongside their bowls, collars, photos with us and the letters. Call me crazy but it made me happy to create a space for them.

I learned during this process that it is illegal in some areas to bury your pet in your backyard. But it's just fine to plant a tree! What better way to memorialize your pet than to plant a tree in his honor? There's an amazing product called BioUrn® that was created when one family just couldn't walk past their dog's ashes another day without falling apart. BioUrn is a biodegradable urn for your dog's ashes that grows into a memorial tree when planted and watered.

*"Maka was our family pet, and our son's constant companion. He even learned how to walk while holding onto Maka. When she crossed the 'Rainbow Bridge,' my whole family was devastated and had trouble processing the loss. Most pet lovers will experience this type of loss since our pets don't live as long as we do. Out of this desire to alleviate our grief, we turned something sad into something beautiful and created a circle of life memorial tree for Maka. Now every time my son goes outside, he tends to 'Maka's tree' which puts a smile on his face."*

—Lisa Brambilla, Creator of BioUrn®
CEO, My Eternal Family Tree®
A Veteran owned, family run business
biournforpets.com

The BioUrn provides comfort after your beloved companion has crossed the Rainbow Bridge, while making the planet a little greener!

*"Humanizing our pets has taken a stronghold on this country. Some might argue that 'dogs are the new kids' is becoming a worldwide trend. Science has finally caught on to what dog lovers have known forever: Dogs have the propensity to feel many of the same emotions humans do.*

*The lifespan of a dog is short—a flicker, if you will, compared with a human's. My dog will pass from this world and leave behind a hole in my heart where it used to be, well, 'whole.' I've been down this road, and I will again and again. How about you?"*

—Carol Bryant, Founder of FidoseofReality.com and
Wigglebutt Warriors®

Best Friends Animal Society hosts a monthly blessing ceremony honoring the memory of animals at the sanctuary who have passed. Visitors are welcome to join and celebrate their beloved pet.

You should also consider who would care for your dog if something unexpected happens to you. Whether you are young and seemingly healthy, or a senior adult adopting a dog, it is a good idea to have a trusted friend or family member lined up to take your dog—someone who knows and loves him and is willing to care for him until the end of his life. There's a lot you can do to ensure your dog's well being when you are unable to care for him.

*"Most pet parents put all their pet care plans in their Will. However, did you know that if you are disabled or become gravely ill, these funds, pet information and plans are not available to you for the care of your pets because you are not dead? Additionally, if you pass away, it can take 6-12 months to read and implement all the terms in your Will. This means your carefully thought out pet-care directives will not be immediately available, which is impractical. Your pets need care right now. One easy solution is to make a MAAP Plan. (The 4 Steps You Need to Take to Navigate Your Pet's Journey When You Cannot Care For Them.) It gives you peace of mind that your pet will receive immediate care, from the moment you face one of the 5 D's-Disaster, Delay, Disability, Disease or Death."*

—Debra Vey Voda-Hamilton, Hamilton Law and Mediation
hamiltonlawandmediation.com

For further details, Debra offers a free webinar.$^{\Delta}$

Before I completed this book Amy Cox shared the following story with me. It blew me away. This is an abridged version of the original.

*"Have you ever had a serendipitous experience? I just did, and my head and heart have not recovered yet.*

*It has been 3 weeks since my precious Paco Man died suddenly, but I still cry everyday. He was my best friend, my constant companion, travel buddy and bedtime snuggler.*

*I looked for things to do that first night, anything to keep me from going to bed. I found myself suddenly swamped with Facebook friend requests from people in the animal rescue world. While scrolling through Facebook that night, a picture of a dog came up, with a posting that said RIP. I read the pet's tribute and commented that I too had lost a pet that day, and wished this person peace. I described my five-pound, black and tan Paco Man and how much he meant to me. I wanted this person to know that a stranger was sharing his pain. By the time I fell asleep I had been up for 36 hours straight.*

*In the morning, there was a comment in the thread that said, "to Amy Cox, please contact the SPCA in McKinney, TX and ask for animal ID # \*\*\*\*\*\*. I called the SPCA and the receptionist explained that this dog was an owner-surrender, weighed almost 5 pounds and was a black and tan Chihuahua. And then she says, "Oh, and his name is Paco." While I am not often at a loss for words, this took my breath away. I knew I was meant to take him home with me, but how could I even consider adding this Paco to our family so soon?*

*I brought him home and that evening, through my tears asked my husband what to do. "Amy, look at this dog, listen to your story. How could you have possibly done anything else but bring him home to us?" He asked what I thought we should call him, and the answer was simple, "Paco Dos."*

*When Paco Dos got into bed with us that night, the very first thing he did was bury himself under the covers, just like Paco Man used to do. Danny looked at me, and I looked at Danny. We didn't need to say anything. Paco Dos was home, and our Paco Man was still with us."*

—Amy Cox, The Paws Cause
www.thepetvet.com


*"At the end of my life—I want my last breath to be taken while I have warm fur under my fingers."*

—Shawna Schuh, President,
Women in the Pet Industry Network
www.womeninthepetindustry.com

# GIVING BACK

*"The greatness of a nation can be judged by the way its animals are treated."*

—Mahatma Gandhi

TWENTY YEARS AGO WE "ACCIDENTALLY" adopted our first dog JJ. He was a gem who opened my heart to loving and being loved by a dog. At that time I learned that between 12 and 16 million potentially adoptable pets were being euthanized annually and I knew that I needed to get involved and help. After all, had we not adopted JJ, he could have been one of those millions.

To create awareness about animal homelessness, I simply started telling people that JJ was a rescued dog. I began to help fundraise for a small non-profit rescue and medical aid group called Animal Guardian Society and served on their board of directors for a number of years, learning all about the rescue and adoption world. As animal rescue garnered more attention, spay and neuter education improved, adoption rates increased and the euthanasia numbers began to drop. There is still more work to do today, as the US euthanasia statistic still lingers in the millions, but it is certainly an improvement. Despite improved numbers in the the US, animal homelessness, abuse and neglect continue to be an international issue. US and international agencies continue to collaborate to educate people and governments about issues like dogfighting, the dogmeat trade and abuse all over the world.

As someone interested in helping animals, or "giving a voice to the voiceless," it is important for me to give back however I can. There are many ways to help, and everyone in my family has gotten involved in animal rescue. My daughter set up a collection for Operation Blankets of Love$^\Delta$ and volunteered at adoption days for Take Me Home Rescue.$^\Delta$ Some adoption agencies allow kids 12 years and older to volunteer supervised. NKLA,$^\Delta$ where my son was able to help care directly for the dogs, just changed their kids and dogs policy so now we primarily volunteer with the cats. I read my children's books to classes and groups, initiate discussions about compassion and responsibility, and donate a percentage of all book proceeds to animal rescue groups.

Now that you have a better understanding of the challenges so many homeless dogs have experienced, you can appreciate the need to support organizations helping the thousands of dogs less fortunate than yours. Besides adopting and caring for a dog, there's even more you can do to give back to the animal community. If you are interested in helping your local shelter or rescue group here are a few things you can do:

- Volunteer your time.
- Walk dogs, socialize cats in a shelter.
- Take up a collection of blankets, food and other needed items for the shelters.
- Photography: Every animal that is up for adoption needs to be photographed and posted online. A

Volunteering in the shelter is a wonderful way to give back but be sure to follow their safety rules, especially if children join you. If you choose to walk dogs at your shelter, only choose the ones you feel you can safely handle.

good photograph of a shelter dog can make all the difference and Shelter Me Photography[Δ] not only takes beautiful photos, but can also teach shelter staff how to take lovely, effective animal photos.

> Many shelters offer Humane Education programs. Find out if your shelter is one of them and learn how you can participate!

- Write descriptions: The more creative (but honest) descriptions help get attention to the animals.
- Donate Money: Perhaps your time is limited but you are in a good financial position to donate. Shelters and rescue organizations can put your money to use right away to help save animals. Check charitynavigator.com to see how the charity you are interested in performs.

> While many kind-hearted people want to rescue every dog they meet, be mindful of your own limitations and remember that if you are not actually starting a sanctuary, you shouldn't over-adopt. You don't want to find yourself in a hoarding situation that ultimately doesn't help anyone.

- Foster: Many rescue organizations rely on foster families. Please see Module 2 for more information.

Adopting dogs in pairs can be great—especially if they are bonded. If you have space, like a home with a big yard or a ranch, consider adopting or fostering multiple pets in need.

## A Note About Dog Fighting and Chaining

In addition to giving back within your community, there are even bigger global issues deserving attention. Perhaps you know people who chain their dog or even engage in dog fighting. While there are laws against dog fighting and chaining, both still exist.

In many parts of the country and world, dogs are still seen as property (or food) rather than companions, and a shift in attitude needs to happen. Thankfully there are organizations making a difference every day.

Excerpted from an article about chaining and tethering$^\Delta$ from the Humane Society of the United States:

"Many dogs still live their lives on the end of a chain or tether. Tied-up outside, dogs become lonely, bored and anxious, and they can develop aggressive behaviors. Bring a dog inside (or help a chained dog in your neighborhood) and you'll keep everyone safer."

Chaining your dog also subjects him to potential taunting by neighborhood kids who don't know any better, and when your dog can't defend himself, he is just a target. Plus, "outside only" dogs are subject to extreme weather conditions. If they are chained up outside, they aren't a bonded part of the family. Finding a loving home for these dogs is much more humane. For more information please read the tips from the HSUS and learn how you can help chained dogs.$^\Delta$

Additionally, dogs suffer greatly in communities where dog fighting is still a prevalent money-making venture. To learn more about dog fighting,$^\Delta$ the HSUS offers a helpful fact sheet. If you suspect or know of any people engaging in dog fighting you can call: 1-877-TIP-HSUS.

*"I expect to pass through this world but once. Any good, therefore, that I can do, or any kindness that I can show to any fellow creature, let me do it now. Let me not defer or neglect it, for I shall not pass this way again."*

—*Stephen Grellet*

When you adopt a homeless dog, you are saving two lives. You are providing a home for that dog and making room in the shelter or rescue organization for another. It is an act of love that gives the dog a chance and gives you the satisfaction of having made a difference. Dogs offer us unconditional love and companionship. They do not judge. They just listen, sit with us and often offer a nuzzle or a kiss exactly when we need it. To honor this relationship we must commit to offering them a chance and the best care possible.

# THANKS FOR READING!

IF YOU HAVE THE TIME, I'd really love a review.
A review would be a huge help, so thank you in advance.

## Wishing you much success with your dog parenting!

I'd love to hear how your dog adoption experience is going
and how else I might be helpful.
Please contact me at info@dianerosesolomon.com

You can go here: www.dianerosesolomon.com
to stay in touch and receive the free infographic I created called
"The Top 10 Ways You Can Help Animals in Your Community
and Beyond Without Breaking the Bank."

Or you can simply send an email to
subscribe@dianerosesolomon.com
to stay tuned for more exciting projects!

More books by Diane Rose-Solomon:

*JJ The American Street Dog and How He Came to Live in Our House*
*JJ Goes to Puppy Class*

# ACKNOWLEDGEMENTS

BIGGEST OF BIG THANK YOUS to Misty Cook for taking this information, brilliantly editing and organizing it so we can now call it a book. It was a pleasure working with you, and your never-ending patience with our unconventional methods was so appreciated.

Thank you Katrina Cantwell for being my right hand woman through SO MUCH of this, slogging through all the stuff that confounded me so I could work on the book. From day one, you've been a "yes" woman, which is a remarkable trait you possess. You are a delight to work with and I'm happy you are a part of my life.

Thank you Karyn Croteau for picking up the ball and running with it. You are a pro and so willing to figure anything and everything out. So glad we are connected.

Thank you Stephanie Morris for your passion and commitment to rescue, your bravery and how dang "in the know" you are in this business. Thank you for your contributions to this book both direct and indirect.

Thank you to my whole family for your support.

Andy—ever the word man with an eagle editorial eye who always has awesome ideas when I get stuck. You have supported me wholeheartedly since day one and for that I am grateful and love you.

My children, Jamie and Zander for your input (whether or not I ask for it!) and for being oh so understanding while I peck away at my computer day after day. I am proud of the compassionate animal lovers you are and I love you so so much.

My parents, Alfred Rose, Frances Lambert, and David Lambert for always being proud.

My sister Julie Ring for setting the foster example in your community.

My brother Michael Rose for always being supportive.

# ACKNOWLEDGEMENTS

Much gratitude to:

The Women's Council: Janet Ramsey, Barbara Budan, Corinne Pierce, Michal McKeown, Jamie Lewis, Kathy Piper and brother Del Piper for being fantastic sounding boards, my reminders to listen and most importantly for your love. Special thanks to Beca Lewis and Jet Tucker for your leadership and counsel.

Lisette Rotman for your creativity, enthusiasm and fabulously fun artwork.

Chris Costine for finding JJ, and thinking to call us which unbeknownst to me at the time set a big ball of furry love into motion.

Paul Marks for your friendship, limitless generosity and the professional time you more than willingly devote.

Kerri Speck for your committed friendship, your support no matter my hairbrained scheme, and laughing at my stupid jokes... all the time.

Joe Bogdan for not only keeping me in line, helping me cross my t's and dot my i's but for doing it with a lot of heart.

Tammy Arlidge for being willing to pick up the tiny pieces and most importantly your friendship.

Fran Garber for enthusiastically stepping in with a smile, professionalism and integrity.

Kathleen Kaiser for sharing your deep knowledge of the book industry and your eagerness to take on this project.

Nate Myers for your creativity, infinite patience, and beautiful design.

Samantha Goodman who was the first person I knew who knew anything about animal rescue and instilled a sense of love and responsibility in me.

Sonndra May who was the second person I knew who knew anything (and everything!) about animal rescue and shared it with all your heart and soul.

Jeffrey Van Dyk, David and Diane Harrison and Wendy "You Rock" Hart for your life changing guidance. To all the members of the Advanced Advanced Advanced Clean Language class—Ana Lisa Hale, Chiarastella Feder, Marlisse Bachrach, Debbie Gador, Helen May, Ilyas M., It has been an honor working and growing with you. Thank you for sharing your metaphors, bravery and friendship with me.

To Jenny La Fontaine for being a gem, a doll and an angel. Yep—all three and then some.

To Delle Norman Griffin for your loving commitment to all animals.

To Karen Rosen for your friendship and knowing so dang much about everything!

To Nicole Gallardo. Thank you for always being willing, and loving my dogs as much as you do.

To Justine Briseno for having the biggest of hearts and showing the world what doing the right thing looks like even in times of extreme adversity.

To Shawna Schuh for exemplifying leadership, empowerment, growth, professionalism, generosity of spirit, and enthusiasm. You have shown me and countless others how much more you get back when you give. You have demonstrated, with your top down approach how women can bolster one another in a supportive environment. Women in the Pet Industry Network rocks and we are all better people for being a part of it. Oh, and I can't think of too many other people who could get me out of bed and onto a conference call at 5am everyday.

Speaking of 5am… Thank you to the 5:15am crew for inspiring me bright and early. You all help me shape the way I think.

Lisa Hacken for having laser eyes, great ideas, a gentle nature, and always being willing to help. Unsolicited.

Melissa and Mars Sandoval for your open hearts, crazy amazing creativity and willingness to do… anything!

Andrea Vecchione for being my biggest cheerleader. Period.

Kathleen Gage for your brilliance, encouragement and leading by example.

Virginia Schifiano Hamilton for being a champion for children and animals.

Faith Foss and TJ Mahar for your friendship, your partnership and for being willing to adopt… well just about everyone.

Julie and Tony Bardin for your love and support.

Jennifer Fischman for your lifelong friendship and enduring Stevie way back when despite your allergies.

Karen Dishner for always being there. I mean always.

Leslie Berger and Paul Williams for your friendship and contribution.

Extra special thanks to Denise Fleck for all of the info you shared with me before, during and after your Pet First Aid and CPR class and your very loving carte blanche to share it in this book as appropriate. Your energy and enthusiasm for everything you do is contagious. You have a giant heart and are a wonderfully supportive friend.

And to everyone who contributed your experience and expertise, I am so grateful you allowed me to use your words: Natalie and Max Stone, Jeannette Hartman, Carolyn Shadle, Stephen M. Hamm, Daniel and Griselda Mayorga, Mona Straub, Beth Larsen, Arthur Jeon, Leah Lessard, Katrina and Jim Cantwell, Rachel Marie Sheppard, Cara Schepps, Reem Regina Tatar, Sam Bryant, Jeni Ellis Halliday, Candace Modrell, Lorien Clemens, Maggie Marton, Kelley Kemp, Kimberly Gauthier, Lisa Iszard, Veronica Glynn, Cindy Dunston Quirk, Leela Ruiz, Carole Feeny, Kristin Waters, Erin Provancha, Kelly Syers, Josh Raphaelson, Elena Volnova, Elyse Horvath, Jen deHaan, Carol Bryant, Leah Hatley, Justine Schuurmans, Robin Bennett, Lynn Medlin, Jody Miller-Young, Leah Hutchison Pacitto, Dawn Celapino, Tricia Montgomery, Beth Stultz, Mike Linville, Amber Kirsten-Smit, Andy Smit, Amy Burkert, Vicki Rae Thorne, Dr. Christina Chambreau, Beke Lubeach, Arden Moore, Tina Kenny, Dr. Jessica Waldman, Sara Henderson, Judy Helm Wright, Lisa Brambilla, Debra Vey Voda-Hamilton, Amy Cox.

Thank you to all the organizations and individual contributors who shared your work in this book. Thank you to Petfinder.com and Adopt-a-pet.com for pairing the technology of the Internet with a love of animals. You are incredible resources for anyone searching for their perfect pet or desiring to be more educated about pets and pet parenting.

Very special acknowledgment to the families who contributed to this book whose dogs have passed or fallen ill since you shared your story with me. Not only does your best friend's love live in your heart, but a little bit of it is now shared with everyone who is touched by this book.

So grateful to everyone who contributed to this book whether your name appears above or not, whether you realize you did or not. You make a difference to Pets, People and the Planet.

Special thanks to Nanette Martin and Pamela Hill from Shelter Me Photography for your gorgeous photos and dedication to making a difference to all animals.

Shelter Me Photography takes professional portraits of shelter animals helping to increase adoption rates. Shelter Me Photography is a not-for-profit organization dedicated to changing the way people view shelter animals through compelling, professional photographs.

# LIST OF ARTICLE LINKS, ORGANIZATIONS AND PRODUCTS BY MODULE

## Module 1:

https://www.avma.org/public/YourVet/Pages/Financial-assistance-for-veterinary-care-costs.aspx

aspca.org Please see dianerosesolomon.com/links for table with projected annual costs.

https://habri.org/docs/HABRI_Report_-_Healthcare_Cost_Savings_from_Pet_Ownership_.pdf

http://www.adoptapet.com/blog/puppy-manual/

http://www.adoptapet.com/blog/hypo-allergenic-dogs-whats-true-whats-not/

http://www.adoptapet.com/blog/reduce-allergies-to-pets/

http://moderndogmagazine.com/articles/what-it-about-pit-bulls/17294

https://www.animallaw.info/article/breed-specific-legislation-united-states

http://www.adoptapet.com/dog-breedshttp://www.adoptapet.com/dog-breeds

## Module 2:

http://www.pet360.com/dog/adoption/kill-shelters-vs-low-kill-and-no-kill-shelters/eC_zmPaWME-mF0Gn95SijQ

www.dachshundrescuesouthflorida.com/

http://bestfriends.org/

Petfinder.com

Adoptapet.com

http://www.ny-petrescue.org

https://www.petfinder.com/animal-shelters-and-rescues/fostering-dogs/

www.PetHub.com

http://www.findingrover.com/

http://mykidhaspaws.org/2015/11/what-should-you-do-when-you-see-a-stray-dog/

http://fearfuldogs.com/how-to-greet-dogs/

http://www.vetstreet.com/our-pet-experts/why-outdoor-dogs-are-miserable

http://www.petmd.com/dog/care/evr_dg_purebred_dogs_complications

puppymillawareness.com

www.aspca.org Please see dianerosesolomon.com/links for more information from ASPCA about puppy mills

http://scgrrescue.org/#sthash.tnUN0nu6.dpbs

http://www.petmd.com/blogs/thedailyvet/ken-tudor/2014/april/dog-bite-fatalities-breed-or-human-problem-31529

http://downtowndogrescue.org/programs/shelter-intervention-program/

http://www.pawsla.org/

http://www.humanesociety.org/issues/pet_overpopulation/facts/why_spay_neuter.html

http://startrescue.org/

## Module 3:

http://www.adoptapet.com/blog/pet-proofing-your-home-101/

walkntrain http://www.coastalpet.com/products/product/wthh1.aspx?style=06100

http://dogtowndogtraining.com

http://blog.betternaturedogtraining.com/2014/01/27/head-collars/

http://healthypets.mercola.com/sites/healthypets/archive/2014/06/11/retractable-dog-leash.aspx

http://www.boomerangtags.com/

https://www.pethub.com/article/pet-theft-prevention-its-fashionable

http://ohmydogblog.com/2014/01/what-should-i-feed-my-dog/

http://www.petmd.com/blogs/fullyvetted/2007/april/bloat-dogs-every-large-breed-owners-worst-nightmare%C2%A6and-mine-too-6032#

http://www.centralfloridaanimaler.com/2013/11/08/healthy-weight/

http://www.ahvma.org/

http://www.reviews.com/dog-food/

http://pets.webmd.com/ask-pet-health-11/dog-feeding

https://www.kongcompany.com/products/

http://biobagusa.com/products/retail-products/pet-waste-products-retail/

http://outwardhound.com/shop/dog-gear/pooch-pickups

http://www.earthrated.com/en/products/

http://www.adoptapet.com/blog/how-to-crate-train-your-puppy-or-dog/

https://www.pethub.com/content/animal-rescuers-perspective-pet-safety

http://www.adoptapet.com/blog/creating-a-dog-friendly-backyard

http://www.ansci.cornell.edu/plants/dogs/

http://naturallyitsclean.com/

http://tucsondogdoors.com/benefits-of-pet-doors/

http://www.petmd.com/blogs/fullyvetted/2010/june/titering_or_vaccines-10182

https://www.petfinder.com/dogs/dog-health/common-dog-skin-problems-intro/

http://www.petmd.com/dog/wellness/evr_multi_flea_control#.

http://www.petmd.com/dog/parasites/evr_dg_10_ways_to_stop_ticks_from_biting_your_dog?page=2

https://www.petfinder.com/dogs/dog-health/common-dog-skin-problems-intro/

https://www.greenies.com/dogs/pill-pockets.aspx

www.aspca.org Please see dianerosesolomon.com/links for more information from ASPCA about low cost spay and neuter.

http://www.dogingtonpost.com/five-phone-numbers-every-dog-owner-should-have-handy/

http://www.petmd.com/dog/grooming/dogs-hair-knots-how-get-them-untangled-and-under-control

https://www.petfinder.com/dogs/dog-grooming/tips-for-tackling-dog-smells/

https://apdt.com/

## Module 4:

http://amandafoundation.org/

http://www.adoptapet.com/blog/teach-your-dog-or-puppy-to-walk-on-leash/

http://www.adoptapet.com/blog/introducing-your-new-dog-to-other-dogs/

http://www.adoptapet.com/blog/6-steps-to-introduce-a-new-cat-to-your-dog/

http://ohmydogblog.com/?s=the+newt+plan&submit

http://www.adoptapet.com/blog/housetraining-your-dog-or-puppy/

http://www.thefamilydog.com/

http://stopthe77.com

http://www.doggonesafe.com/

http://www.robinkbennett.com/

http://www.adoptapet.com/blog/dog-training-tip-teach-your-dog-to-greet-guests-politely-instead-of-jumping-up/

http://familypaws.com/fpaw/wp-content/uploads/2011/10/FPPE-Dog-Baby-Sheet-sm.pdf

http://www.doggonesafe.com/baby_safety_around_dogs

https://www.avma.org/public/PetCare/Pages/Cold-weather-pet-safety.aspx

http://www.ansci.cornell.edu/plants/dogs/

https://www.pethub.com/article/your-pet-vs-4th-july-fire-works-infographic

www.aspca.org Please see dianerosesolomon.com/links for more information from ASPCA about Halloween safety tips

https://apdt.com/

http://dogtowndogtraining.com/

http://www.patriciamcconnell.com/store/Feisty-Fido.html

http://barkandswagger.com/shelter-stars-hows-jasper-hes-found-his-calling-as-a-tropical-terrier

http://www.dogingtonpost.com/what-every-dog-owner-should-know-about-foxtails/

https://www.petfinder.com/dogs/dog-training/i-pull-you-pull/

http://k9fitclub.com/

https://www.pethub.com/content/tips-dog-friendly-hiking-info-graphic-0

**Module 5:**

www.fidofunwalks.com

https://www.petsit.com/

https://www.pethub.com/content/preparing-pet-sitter

http://www.pet-service-directory.com/

http://www.adoptapet.com/blog/help-your-dog-stop-crying-when-left-alone/

http://www.adoptapet.com/blog/how-to-keep-a-dog-off-kitchen-counters/

http://dogtv.com/

http://www.gopetfriendly.com/

http://www.petswelcome.com/

http://sleepypod.com/clickit

http://pupsaver.com/

http://petfriendlyrestaurants.com/

http://www.akc.org/dog-owners/training/canine-good-citizen/what-is-canine-good-citizen/

http://bestfriends.org/sanctuary/explore-sanctuary/dogtown/vicktory-dogs

# LIST OF ARTICLE LINKS, ORGANIZATIONS AND PRODUCTS BY MODULE

http://bestfriends.org/

https://freedomservicedogs.org/

https://petpartners.org/volunteer/our-therapy-animal-program/

https://petpartners.org/volunteer/become-a-handler/

http://thegooddogfoundation.org/

bideawee.org/

https://petpartners.org/

http://www.dogsoncall.org/

http://www.animalhavenshelter.org/

http://www.usdaa.com/

http://www.k9nosework.com

https://www.avma.org/News/JAVMANews/Pages/091001c.aspx

www.calanimalrehab.com

http://helpemup.com/

http://www.solvitproducts.com/

http://solutions.blair.com/e/vista-rugs-stair-treads/8098.uts

http://www.caninerehabinstitute.com

http://ohmydogblog.com/2015/08/on-cancer-and-kindness/

http://vetspecialists.com/

http://www.ahvma.org/

www.consumersadvocate.org/pet-insurance/best-pet-insurance

http://sunnydogink.com/

http://petfirstaid4u.com/

http://blogpaws.com/

http://snarranimalrescue.org/home.html

https://deafdogsrock.com/

http://www.halosforpaws.com/

aspca.org article: Please visit dianerosesolomon.com/links to learn more about the rehabilitation program for abused and neglected dogs from the ASPCA

http://www.beaglefreedomproject.org/

## Rehoming:

http://www.adoptapet.com/blog/how-can-i-find-a-new-home-for-my-pet/

## Saying Goodbye:

http://www.choicevet.com/

http://www.hopeveterinarycenter.org/

www.deathofmypet.com

http://biourn4pets.com/

http://hamiltonlawandmediation.com/proactive-pet-parents-webinar/

www.thepetvet.com

## Giving Back:

http://www.operationblanketsoflove.org/

http://takemehome.tv/

http://nkla.org/

https://www.facebook.com/ShelterMePhoto/

http://www.humanesociety.org/

http://www.humanesociety.org/issues/chaining_tethering/tips/help_chained_dogs.html

http://www.humanesociety.org/issues/dogfighting/facts/dogfighting_fact_sheet.html?credit=web_id85537499

# LINKS TO CONTRIBUTORS AND THEIR COMPANY OR ORGANIZATION

Robin Bennett
www.robinkbennett.com
Lisa Brambilla, BioUrn®
www.biourn4pets.com
Carol Bryant, Fidose of Reality
www.fidoseofreality.com
Amy Burkert, Go Pet Friendly
www.gopetfriendly.com
Dawn Celapino, Leash Your Fitness
www.leashyourfitness.com
Dr. Christina Chambreau, DVM
www.christinachambreau.com
Lorien Clemens, Pet Hub
www.pethub.com
Amy Cox, The Paws Cause
www.thepetvet.com
Jen deHaan, Found Pixel
www.foundpixel.com
Carole Feeny and Kristin Waters, Project Blue Collar
www.projectbluecollar.com
Denise Fleck, Sunny-dog Ink,
www.sunnydogink.com
Kimberly Gauthier, Keep the Tail Wagging
www.keepthetailwagging.com

Jeni Ellis Halliday, Halli-Loo™
    Halli-Loo.com
Virginia Schifiano Hamilton, Canine Commandos
    caninecommandos.com
Debra Vey Voda-Hamilton, Hamilton Law and Mediation
    www.hamiltonlawandmediation.com
Steve M. Hamm, Sweetwater Valley Dog Rescue
    https://www.sweetwatervalleyrescue.com
Jeannette Hartman, Fido Universe
    www.fidouniverse.com
Leah Hatley and Justine Schuurmans, The Family Dog
    www.thefamilydog.com
Sara Henderson, BOGO Bowl
    www.bogobowl.com
Elyse Horvath, Natural Paws
    www.naturalpaws.net
Lisa Iszard, Tumbleweed and Eddies
    http://www.tumbleweedandeddies.com
Arthur Jeon and Leah Lessard, Global Animal
    www.globalanimal.org
Kelley Kemp, Bakersfield Dog Behavior
    www.bakersfielddogbehavior.com
Tina Kenny, TLC Pet Sitting, LA Based Pet Sitter
    tlc4pets@msn.com
Amber Kirsten-Smit & Andy Smit, Swiftpet™
    www.swiftpet.com
Beth Larsen, Waggletops®
    www.waggletops.com
Mike Linville, Black Dog Marketing
    Pet-Service-Directory.com
Beke Lubeach, Dog Bone Marketing Solutions
    www.dogbonemarketing.com
Nanette Martin, Shelter Me Photography
    www.facebook.com/sheltermephoto/
Maggie Marton, Oh My Dog Blog
    www.ohmydogblog.com

Lynn Medlin, Dog Town Dog Training
http://dogtowndogtraining.com
Jody Miller-Young, Bark & Swagger
www.barkandswagger.com
Candace Modrell, Shelter Transport Animal Rescue Team (S.T.A.R.T)
www.startrescue.org
Tricia Montgomery, K-9 Fit Club
http://k9fitclub.com/
Arden Moore, Pet First Aid 4 U
petfirstaid4u.com
Leah Hutchison Pacitto, Dog Gone Good Dog Training
www.doggonegooddogtraining.com
Erin Provancha, Tucson Dog Doors,
www.tucsondogdoors.com
Cindy Dunston Quirk, Scout & Zoe's Antler Chews
www.scoutandzoes.com
Leela Ruiz, Dog and House
www.dogandhouse.com
Shawna Schuh, Women in the Pet Industry Network
www.womeninthepetindustry.com
Carolyn Shadle, PH.D, Veterinarian Communication
www.veterinariancommunication.com
Rachel Marie Sheppard, My Kid Has Paws
www.mykidhaspaws.org
Mona Straub, Just Fur Fun
www.justfurfunonline.com
Beth Stultz, Pet Sitters International
https://www.petsit.com
Reem Regina Tatar, Puppy Mill Awareness
www.puppymillawareness.com
Vicki Rae Thorne, Earth Heart °Inc.,
www.earthheartinc.com
Elena Volnova, Dog Fashion Spa
www.dogfashion.us

Dr. Jessica Waldman, VMD, CVA, CCRT
California Animal Rehabilitation (CARE)
www.calanimalrehab.com
Judy Helm Wright, Death of My Pet
www.deathofmypet.com

# BIBLIOGRAPHY

Adopt a Pet™. "The Puppy Manual from Adopt-a-Pet.com". Accessed May 3, 2016. <http://www.adoptapet.com/blog/puppy-manual/>.

Adopt a Pet™. "Hypo-Allergenic Dogs: What's True What's Not", September 10, 2010. Accessed May 3, 2016. <http://www.adoptapet.com/blog/hypo-allergenic-dogs-whats-true-whats-not/>.

Adopt a Pet™. "What Dog Breed is Best for You?". Accessed May 3, 2016. <http://www.adoptapet.com/dog-breeds>.

Adopt a Pet™. "Creating a Dog Friendly Back Yard", July 27, 2010. Accessed May 3, 2016. <http://www.adoptapet.com/blog/creating-a-dog-friendly-backyard>.

Adopt a Pet™. "Housetraining Your Dog or Puppy", November 29, 2010. Accessed May 4, 2016. <http://www.adoptapet.com/blog/housetraining-your-dog-or-puppy/>.

Adopt a Pet™. May 27, 2015, "Dog Training Tip: Teach Your Dog to Greet Guests Politely (Instead of Jumping Up)". Accessed May 4, 2016. <http://www.adoptapet.com/blog/dog-training-tip-teach-your-dog-to-greet-guests-politely-instead-of-jumping-up/>.

Adopt a Pet™. August 11, 2014, "How Can I Find a New Home for My Pet?". Accessed May 5, 2016 <http://www.adoptapet.com/blog/how-can-i-find-a-new-home-for-my-pet/>.

AKC-American Kennel Club. "About Canine Good Citizen: What Is It?". Accessed May 5, 2016. <http://www.akc.org/dog-owners/training/canine-good-citizen/what-is-canine-good-citizen/>.

ARME'S Beagle Freedom Project. *Beaglefreedomproject.org*. Accessed May 6, 2016. <http://www.beaglefreedomproject.org/>.

Arnold, Brandy. "5 Phone Numbers Every Dog Owner Should Have Handy", September 1, 2015. *dogingtonpost.com*. Accessed May 4, 2016. <http://www.dogingtonpost.com/five-phone-numbers-every-dog-owner-should-have-handy/>.

Arnold, Brandy. "What Every Dog Owner Should Know About Foxtails", July 14, 2015. *dogingtonpost.com*. Accessed May 9, 2016. <http://www.dogingtonpost.com/what-every-dog-owner-should-know-about-foxtails/>.

AVMA™. "Financial Assistance for Veterinary Care Costs". Accessed May 9, 2016. <https://www.avma.org/public/YourVet/Pages/Financial-assistance-for-veterinary-care-costs.aspx >.

AVMA™. "Cold Weather Pet Safety". Accessed May 9, 2016 <https://www.avma.org/public/PetCare/Pages/Cold-weather-pet-safety.aspx>.

AVMA™. "Pet Rehab Becoming Mainstream Practice". Accessed May 27, 2016 <https://www.avma.org/News/JAVMANews/Pages/091001c.aspx>.

Becker, Karen, PhD. "Why I Don't Recommend Retractable Collars", June 11, 2014. *Healthypets.mercola.com*. Accessed May 3, 2016. <http://healthypets.mercola.com/sites/healthypets/archive/2014/06/11/retractable-dog-leash.aspx>.

Best Friends®. "The Brave, Beautiful Dogs Out of Bad Newz Kennel". Accessed May 5, 2016. <http://bestfriends.org/sanctuary/explore-sanctuary/dogtown/vicktory-dogs>.

Burkert, Amy. "Infographic: Tips for Dog Friendly Hiking", June 11, 2014. *gopetfriendlyblog.com*. Accessed May 21, 2016. <http://www.gopetfriendlyblog.com/infographic-tips-for-dog-friendly-hiking/>.

Cornell University Department of Animal Science. "Poisonous Plants Affecting Dogs". *Cornell.edu*. Accessed May 4, 2016. <http://poisonousplants.ansci.cornell.edu/dogs/>.

Cower, Terry L., PhD and Neaves, Tonya T., PhD. "The Healthcare Cost Savings from Pet Ownership". *habri.org*. Accessed May 3, 2016. <http://habri.org/docs/HABRI_Report_-_Healthcare_Cost_Savings_from_Pet_Ownership_.pdf>

Davis, Andrea. "Pet Proofing Your Home 101", November 21, 2014. *adoptapet.com*. Accessed May 3, 2016. <http://www.adoptapet.com/blog/pet-proofing-your-home-101/>.

Doggonesafe. "Baby Safety Around Dogs". Accessed May 4, 2016. <http://www.doggonesafe.com/baby_safety_around_dogs>.

Feeny, Carole and Waters, Kristin. "From The Animal Rescuer's Perspective on Pet Safety". *pethub.com*. Accessed May 27, 2016. <https://www.pethub.com/content/animal-rescuers-perspective-pet-safety>.

Frosek, Rose. "What Is It About Pit Bulls?". *Modern Dog Magazine*. Accessed May 8, 2016. <http://moderndogmagazine.com/articles/what-it-about-pit-bulls/17294>.

Gillaspy, Eric, CPDT-KA. "I Pull, You Pull". Accessed May 4, 2016. <https://www.petfinder.com/dogs/dog-training/i-pull-you-pull/>.

Jacobs, Debbie. "How to Greet Dogs". *fearfuldogs.com*. Accessed May 3, 2016. <http://fearfuldogs.com/how-to-greet-dogs/>.

Kelly, Jackie. "Kill Shelters vs. Low Kill and No Kill Shelters". *pet360.com*. Accessed May 3, 2016. <http://www.pet360.com/dog/adoption/kill-shelters-vs-low-kill-and-no-kill-shelters/eC_zmPaWME-mF0Gn95SijQ>.

Khuly, Patty, PhD. "Every Large Breed Owner's Worst Nightmare and Mine Too", April 22, 2007. *petMD.com*. Accessed May 3, 2016. <http://www.petmd.com/blogs/fullyvetted/2007/april/bloat-dogs-every-large-breed-owners-worst-nightmare%C2%A6and-mine-too-6032>.

Khuly, Patty, PhD. "The Truth Behind Titering Instead of Vaccinations", June 28, 2010. *petMD.com*. Accessed May 4, 2016. <http://www.petmd.com/blogs/fullyvetted/2010/june/titering_or_vaccines-10182>.

Kvamme, Jennifer, DVM. "10 Ways to Remove a Tick from a Dog". *petMD.com*. Accessed May 4, 2016. <http://www.petmd.com/dog/parasites/evr_dg_10_ways_to_stop_ticks_from_biting_your_dog?page=2>.

Marton, Maggie. "What Should I Feed My Dog". Oh My Dog Blog. Accessed May 27, 2016. <http://ohmydogblog.com/2014/01/what-should-i-feed-my-dog/>.

Marton, Maggie. "The Newt Plan: Introducing Dogs and Cats". *Oh My Dog Blog*. Accessed May 27, 2016. <http://ohmydogblog.com/?s=the+newt+plan&submit>.

Marton, Maggie. "On Cancer and Kindness". Oh My Dog Blog. Accessed May 27, 2016. <http://ohmydogblog.com/2015/08/on-cancer-and-kindness/>.

Miller-Young, Jody. "Shelter Stars—How's Jasper? He's Found His Calling as a Tropical Terrier". *barkandswagger.com*. Accessed May 27, 2016. <http://barkandswagger.com/shelter-stars-hows-jasper-hes-found-his-calling-as-a-tropical-terrier>.

Petfinder™. "Fostering Dogs". Accessed May 3, 2016. <https://www.petfinder.com/animal-shelters-and-rescues/fostering-dogs/>.

Petfinder™. "What's that Smell? Tips for Tackling Dog Smells". *PetFinder's The Adopted Dog Bible*. Accessed May 27, 2016. <https://www.petfinder.com/dogs/dog-grooming/tips-for-tackling-dog-smells/>.

PetHub. "Pet Theft Prevention: It's Fashionable!". *Pethub.com.* Accessed July 17, 2016 <https://www.pethub.com/article/pet-theft-prevention-its-fashionable/>.

PetHub. "Your Pet Vs. 4th July Fire Works (Infographic)". *PetHub.com.* Accessed July 17, 2016. < https://www.pethub.com/article/your-pet-vs-4th-july-fire-works-infographic>

PetMD. "Problems Common to Purebred Dogs". Accessed May 3, 2016. <http://www.petmd.com/dog/care/evr_dg_purebred_dogs_complications>.

PetMD. "Natural Home Remedies for Flea and Tick Control". Accessed May 27, 2016. <http://www.petmd.com/dog/wellness/evr_multi_flea_control#>.

PetMD. "Dog's Hair in Knots? How to Get Them Untangled and Under Control". Accessed May 27, 2016 <http://www.petmd.com/dog/grooming/dogs-hair-knots-how-get-them-untangled-and-under-control>.

Pet Partners. "Our Therapy Animal Program". Accessed May 27, 2016. <https://petpartners.org/volunteer/our-therapy-animal-program/>.

Pet Partners. "Become a Handler". Accessed May 27, 2016. <https://petpartners.org/volunteer/become-a-handler/>.

Reeves, Jessica. "Is Your Dog at a Healthy Weight?", November 8, 2013. *centralfloridaanimaler.com.* Accessed May 3, 2016. <http://www.centralfloridaanimaler.com/2013/11/08/healthy-weight/>.

Reviews.com. "Best Dog Food. It's All About Quality Ingredients: Best Food for a Safe and Happy Dog", July 14, 2015. Accessed May 3, 2016. <http://www.reviews.com/dog-food>.

Saling, Joseph. "Feeding Tips for Dogs", August 2011. *WebMD.com.* Accessed May 3, 2016. <http://pets.webmd.com/ask-pet-health-11/dog-feeding>.

Sellers, Jennnifer. "Dog Skin Problems: Introduction". *Pet MD.com.* Accessed May 4, 2016. <https://www.petfinder.com/dogs/dog-health/common-dog-skin-problems-intro/>.

Sheppard, Rachel Marie. "What Should You Do When You See a Stray Dog?". *mykidhaspaws.org.* Accessed May 27, 2016. <http://mykidhaspaws.org/2015/11/what-should-you-do-when-you-see-a-stray-dog/>.

Shyrock, Jennifer. "Dog and Baby Safety", October 2011. *familypaws.com.* Accessed May 8, 2016. <http://familypaws.com/fpaw/wp-content/uploads/2011/10/FPPE-Dog-Baby-Sheet-sm.pdf>.

Spofadori, Gina. "Why Outdoor Dogs Are Miserable", July 5, 2011. *vetstreet.com.* Accessed May 3, 2016. <http://www.vetstreet.com/our-pet-experts/why-outdoor-dogs-are-miserable>.

Stallings, Jeff. "Head Collars for Loose Leash Walking", January 27, 2014. *betterna-turedogtraining.com*. Accessed May 3, 2016. <http://blog.betternaturedogtrain-ing.com/2014/01/27/head-collars/>.

The Humane Society of the United States. "Why You Should Spay/Neuter Your Pet". Accessed May 23, 2016. <http://www.humanesociety.org/issues/pet_overpopu-lation/facts/why_spay_neuter.html>.

The Humane Society of the United States. "Chaining and Tethering". Accessed May 5, 2016. <http://www.humanesociety.org/issues/chaining_tethering/>.

The Humane Society of the United States. "Chaining and Tethering Dogs: Frequenty Asked Questions". Accessed May 27, 2016. <http://www.humanesociety.org/issues/chaining_tethering/facts/chaining_tethering_facts.html?credit=web_id80866531>.

The Humane Society of the United States. "Dogfighting Fact Sheet". Accessed May 5, 2016 <http://www.humanesociety.org/issues/dogfighting/facts/dogfighting_fact_sheet.html?credit=web_id85537499>.

Tudor, Ken, PhD. "Dog Bite Fatalities: Breed or Human Problem?". April 3, 2014. *PetMD.com*. Accessed May 3, 2016. <http://www.petmd.com/blogs/thedaily-vet/ken-tudor/2014/april/dog-bite-fatalities-breed-or-human-problem-31529>.

Warner, Jennifer. "Teach Your Dog or Puppy to Walk on Leash", May 10, 2011. *adoptapet.com*. Accessed May 4, 2016. <http://www.adoptapet.com/blog/teach-your-dog-or-puppy-to-walk-on-leash/>.

Warner Jacobsen, Jennifer. "Tips to Reduce Allergies to Pets", June 8, 2010. *adopta-pet.com*. Accessed May 3, 2016. <http://www.adoptapet.com/blog/reduce-aller-gies-to-pets/>.

Warner Jacobsen, Jennifer. "How to Crate Train Your Puppy or Dog", October 21, 2010. *adoptapet.com*. Accessed May 3, 2016. <http://www.adoptapet.com/blog/how-to-crate-train-your-puppy-or-dog/>.

Warner Jacobsen, Jennifer. "Introducing Your New Dog to Other Dogs", February 14, 2011. *adoptapet.com*. Accessed May 4, 2016. <http://www.adoptapet.com/blog/introducing-your-new-dog-to-other-dogs/>.

Warner Jacobsen, Jennifer. "6 Steps to Introduce a New Cat to Your Dog", January 5, 2010. *adoptapet.com*. Accessed May 4, 2016. <http://www.adoptapet.com/blog/6-steps-to-introduce-a-new-cat-to-your-dog/>.

Warner Jacobsen, Jennifer. "Help Your Dog Stop Crying When Left Alone", July 6, 2011. *adoptapet.com*. Accessed May 4, 2016. <http://www.adoptapet.com/blog/help-your-dog-stop-crying-when-left-alone/>.

Warner Jacobsen, Jennifer. "How to Keep a Dog off Kitchen Counters", February 28, 2012. *adoptapet.com*. Accessed May 4, 2016. <http://www.adoptapet.com/blog/how-to-keep-a-dog-off-kitchen-counters/>.

Weiss, Linda S. "Breed Specific Legislation in the United States". *Michigan State University College of Law, 2001; Animal Legal and Historical Center*. Accessed May 3, 2016. <https://www.animallaw.info/article/breed-specific-legislation-united-states>.

# INDEX